A
SILENCED
VOICE

A
SILENCED
VOICE

THE LIFE OF
JOURNALIST KIM WALL

INGRID & JOACHIM WALL

TRANSLATED BY KATHY SARANPA

 AMAZON **CROSSING**

Previously published as *Boken om Kim Wall* by Albert Bonniers Förlag in Sweden in 2018. Translated from Swedish by Kathy Saranpa. First published in English by Amazon Crossing in 2020.

Published by Amazon Crossing, Seattle
www.apub.com

Amazon, the Amazon logo, and Amazon Crossing are trademarks of Amazon.com, Inc., or its affiliates.

ISBN-13: 9781542018111 (hardcover)
ISBN-10: 1542018110 (hardcover)
ISBN-13: 9781542018142 (paperback)
ISBN-10: 1542018145 (paperback)

Cover design by Jarrod Taylor
Cover photography by Tom Wall

All photos are courtesy of the authors.

Printed in the United States of America

First edition

In memory of Kim Wall
1987–2017

AUTHORS' NOTE

In August 2017, our daughter, Kim, was murdered aboard a homemade submarine while she was on an interview assignment. We found ourselves in a maelstrom of incomprehensible events and grief—but also, unbelievably, much warmth, love, and joy. Writing this book about Kim has been a healing journey. We've had long hours of crying as we've remembered the thirty years we had Kim here with us and mourned the many years with her we've been cheated of, but we've had plenty of laughter as well. We've also gotten to know many people around the world—Kim's friends as well as strangers who have been affected by Kim's fate. Our goal—to help Kim's memory live on and to make her a model for other young women—is what keeps us going. The Kim Wall Memorial Fund has already sent four young women journalists out into the world to report in Kim's name and spirit—reporters who give a voice to people who normally don't have one. As Kim did. The work with the fund brings us comfort. Kim will not be remembered as a crime victim: She'll be remembered for a long, long time as the highly qualified journalist and wonderful woman she was.

To learn more about the Kim Wall Memorial Fund, visit the Kim Wall Memorial Fund page on Facebook, the website www.remembering -kimwall.com, or the website of the International Women's Media Foundation (www.iwmf.org/programs/kim-wall-memorial-fund).

CHAPTER 1

The quiet of our bedroom is pierced by a ringing phone. The red numbers projected on the ceiling show 5:31 a.m. It's Friday morning, August 11, 2017. I answer the phone while Jocke, lying next to me in bed, remains asleep. The voice on the other end of the line belongs to Ole, Kim's partner. He sounds shaken, his voice is forced, and he asks if it's OK if we speak English. Ole is afraid we won't understand each other. Although it's less than thirty miles between Trelleborg, Sweden, and Copenhagen, Denmark, it's not always possible for a Swede and a Dane to understand each other. But what he has to say can't be misunderstood: "Kim has disappeared from a submarine near Copenhagen." If there hadn't been such obvious worry in his voice, I would have thought he was kidding. Disappeared? From a submarine? Near Copenhagen? This is how the nightmare began—the nightmare we would never awaken from. Our daughter, sister, and sweetheart left to do an interview for a story—a completely ordinary workday for a freelance journalist. But Kim never came home from work. Instead of writing headlines, she became one.

I wake Jocke. We ask Ole if we can call him back. Soon we're completely awake, and ever so slowly, a completely improbable picture takes shape. Our daughter left yesterday evening to do a story about a man well known in Denmark who builds submarines and wants to launch himself into space. Kim was supposed to do the interview on board the *UC3 Nautilus*, which the man had designed and cobbled together himself. The underwater craft was a well-known silhouette in Copenhagen.

Ole says he's stayed up all night waiting for her. He's biked all over Refshale Island in the northern part of Copenhagen, looking for her, calling her cell phone over and over, searching everywhere. He woke up the submarine man's wife to ask what she knows. He's called the police and the Danish Coast Guard. He's pleaded and begged them to understand that this is serious. Ole has done everything in his power to find Kim. She was just going to finish this assignment before meeting up with him and some good friends after work.

We try to get a picture of what might have happened. We decide there's been an accident. Something's happened with the submarine that made it impossible for it to resurface. The fifty-nine-foot-long *UC3 Nautilus*, built from the base of a wind turbine, is lying somewhere on the bottom of Öresund. How do you find a submarine? We picture those helicopters looking for Russian submarines in the Stockholm archipelago in the 1980s. Did they use sonar? Is it difficult, or even possible, to find a boat underwater? How long does the oxygen last? Ole finds out that for two people, the oxygen on board lasts for twelve hours. It's been almost that long since Ole got the most recent text message from Kim: *We're diving now.* The clock is ticking entirely too quickly.

In Denmark, the rescue crews are already working. Jocke calls the Coast Guard, the agency in charge. "We've got a helicopter in the air and three ships out. We're trying to determine where he sailed. We're certain he left the harbor and was in surface position at that time, around 9:30 p.m.," the officer on duty tells Jocke. My husband jots some notes as quickly as he can on a pad so I can follow the conversation. "Oh no," I hear him say, "it's going to be rough—that's a big area to search." The officer in Århus agrees: "You're right. And the boat left Refshale Island hours ago."

Nobody knows where the submarine is. Öresund, the strait between Sweden and Denmark, is wide. The officer has the same information we got earlier from Ole, that the oxygen on board will last for twelve hours. "Time's up pretty soon, then. Only two hours left," Jocke says, the worry in his voice obvious. "True, if they went underwater right away. But we don't have any indication that they're on the bottom. We've tried calling her cell, but we haven't gotten an answer. The police are trying to ping it," the neutral voice informs us.

We learn that they're not using underwater sonar. They're only searching the surface of the ocean.

The Danish military is searching, too, and they've already made contact with the Swedish authorities. "We'll ask for additional assistance if we need it. It's hard to say where to look," says the Coast Guard officer.

This call doesn't ease our fears. The sea is huge, and our daughter is out there somewhere. Finding a boat on the water's surface is difficult enough. In this case, it might also be beneath the waves. We call the Swedish sea rescue forces and police. We hope that more people will get involved. Anything to increase the chances of finding the submarine. We search for information on the internet. We listen to the radio and follow the news on television. It's still early in the morning, but the vanished submarine is the top news. At 7:00 a.m., the Danish media are already reporting the story. One headline reads: "Helicopters and Ships Searching for Private Submarine with Two On Board near Copenhagen." The article briefly reports what is known at this point. As longtime professional newspaper journalists, we find the situation familiar. But this time the unfolding news story is about our daughter, our Kimsan. It's almost impossible to take it in. It feels so completely unreal that if this were a film, you'd turn it off. It's simply nonsense.

This particular Friday, we're supposed to be traveling to Berlin to celebrate the forty-five years we've shared our lives, and the thirty-one years we've been married. We've made this celebratory trip many times before.

We were supposed to make the short drive from Gislöv Beach to the ferry terminal in Trelleborg to sail to Sassnitz. From there, we would drive through eastern Germany to Berlin. The reason we exchanged rings on that day in August 1986 was Kim: She had announced her imminent birth.

For a month, we'd been traveling in the US and the Caribbean. We'd seen the Grand Canyon, lost seventy-five cents gambling in Las Vegas, enjoyed San Francisco, and gone snorkeling in Cozumel. My pregnancy hadn't caused any problems. In fact, I felt fantastic, even as my belly got bigger and more awkward. Finally, we were sitting in uncomfortable plastic chairs at New York's JFK. It was late. My whole body, particularly my feet, was tired, and I couldn't wait to board our flight to Copenhagen. That's when it happened: all of a sudden, a quick little kick in my belly. And then another. Our baby was starting to communicate with us! In the humid terminal, we experienced a wonder. There was a small human being moving around in there, and time stood still.

CHAPTER 2

This time there won't be a ferry ride in late summer sunlight to Berlin. Instead, we're driving across the Öresund Bridge, heading to Copenhagen and Refshale Island. The bags we packed follow along, because we hope and believe that everything will be fine, that Kim will return unharmed and we can resume our anniversary trip, simply driving to the German capital through Denmark. During the drive to Copenhagen, we're fed information through Danish radio stations. The vanished submarine is "breaking news"—the top story in each broadcast. Our worry grows slowly. It seems to take forever to get through traffic—so many red lights, so many commuters in the morning rush hour. At last we reach Refshale Island. There we can see the large helicopter at a distance, hovering over the water. That's when it becomes undeniably real: They're looking for Kim. She's out there somewhere.

At first glance, Refshale Island looks shabby. Once home to the Burmeister & Wain shipyard, its long-gone glory days echo in the dilapidated buildings that are left, now serving as canvases for graffiti artists. Bicycles fill nearly every empty space. Opposite Refshale Island, on the other side of the seaward entrance to Copenhagen, is Langelinie and the famous Little Mermaid. This morning, as on every other morning during the tourist season, buses are lining up in long rows. Everyone wants to see, admire, and take pictures of the mermaid. On this particular weekend, there's a music festival on Refshale Island. Stage crew, scaffold builders, and others are already very busy despite the early hour. Many of them have worked all night to get things ready in time. Someone mistakes us for volunteers and gives us a temporary parking pass.

We meet up with Ole, and together we walk down a few hundred yards to the rusty wharf where the *Nautilus* usually docks. The whole area is in sorry shape. The asphalt is pitted and broken, and the grass grows up through it. There's an obvious lack of care here. In the background, we hear sounds from the big stage that's being built not far from the wharf. Ole points: "That's where the submarine was. I followed Kim part of the way there."

We wander around for a while in the harbor area and keep tabs on all the developments on our cell phones. Ole makes one call after another—we try in vain to get both certainty and information. We have more and more questions, but no answers. The most important of these is how long the oxygen on board will last. The information we get varies: Twelve hours? Twenty-four hours? If there are two on board, do you divide the hours by two? Nobody knows. And how deep is Öresund?

Some larger holes must have been created on the ocean floor when they dug out the sand for the bridge. Can you get out of a submarine if it's that deep underwater? Where's the submarine? Where's Kim? The helicopter whipping up waves in the sea is real; the situation is not.

We're able to express our feelings in text messages to family and close friends: Kim is the one who's disappeared; she's the one they're talking about on the news. Now the Swedish media have also awakened. The name is as yet unknown, but the story itself attracts interest. The media business is still suffering from summer drought, and the combination of vanished submarine and journalist is enough to grab the attention of news editors.

We decide to drive the short way back to the submarine captain's battered hangar on the east side of the peninsula. A sign with the initials "RML" hangs outside the rusty door. Ole's already been here several times during the night and early morning. Some of the inventor's coworkers have gathered near the door. One says he's the manager and tells us he's probably as worried as we are. The submarine is gone, and the manager is anxious about how this is going to affect the image of the business.

The main activity in this old industrial structure is to build spaceships. The man Kim was supposed to interview, who calls himself "Rocket Madsen," is completely convinced that he'll be the first private citizen launched into space in a self-built rocket. The submarine (which, we learn, is not considered a true submarine by many, as it can't be maneuvered underwater, among other deficiencies) will be used as a launchpad for the spacecraft.

His first attempt at a launch was planned for a few weeks from now. Peter Madsen had applied for, and been granted, a permit to send a rocket into space from somewhere in the sea near Bornholm. But for some unknown reason, Madsen decided on Wednesday night, August 9, to postpone the scheduled launch.

Not very far from us, there's an old rocket. It looks more like a leftover prop from a sci-fi movie, but it's a sign that a space competition of an odd sort is feverishly underway. The submarine man's team is competing against another team to launch the first homemade rocket into space.

Suddenly, the phone rings. The submarine has been spotted—everyone on board is fine! We weep for joy, and I feel immense relief. We hug each other when we hear that this news has been confirmed by official sources. These few hours of drama are now over, and I look at the clock to see if there's enough time to get to Berlin at a decent hour. There is, but first I want to hold Kim really tight. Someone yells, "We have radio contact with the sub!" Ole and Jocke go along with the submarine guys to another building. I use the time to send reassuring text messages to those on the other side of Öresund waiting for news. Our son, Tom, works as a photographer for the daily *Helsingborgs Dagblad*, where news about the submarine incident has been buzzing since he arrived for his shift. His immediate supervisor knows that Kim is the missing journalist, but nobody else on the staff does.

We talk on the phone and agree that he should stay at work and that he doesn't need to come to Copenhagen. Everything is fine now— Kim has been saved, she's OK, end of story. Or maybe not: This is a story Kim will enjoy embroidering on with family and friends for a long time to come.

But this is not the end of the story. It's not even the beginning.

Soon Jocke and Ole come back, their eyes filled with worry. The submarine sank, and apparently only one person has been saved. It can't be true—we just heard that they found the submarine and that everyone on board was fine. Where is Kim? She's the one who was saved, right? Terror grips me again. Soon we get word that it was the submarine man who was saved by a pleasure boat in the ocean, not Kim. He'll be brought to land at the harbor near Kastrup Airport, or at Dragør Harbor. We jump into the car and drive, probably entirely too fast, toward Kastrup. The harbor is deserted, so we continue to Dragør. As we drive, we listen to the radio, which is full of news about the submarine incident. There isn't room for anything else now, and there hasn't been all morning. Ole makes one call after another to try to clarify what's happened. So many contradictory statements; our uncertainty is total.

Dragør is known as an idyllic little harbor with dock restaurants that serve the ferry guests. Today, we're met by a crowd of journalists and photographers.

Teams of reporters are filming and doing stand-ups before cameras, following every event in the harbor. We move away toward the large gray-green helicopter that is getting ready for takeoff. Jocke tries in vain to convince a policeman to stop the helicopter: "Kim is still out there—you have to keep looking for her!"

The submarine man is sitting in one of the police cars. We can see his silhouette through the window. A few minutes earlier he had reached land, smiling and showing a thumbs-up to the waiting reporters, saying that everything was OK. Yes, he's a little sad because his submarine sank, but "she's insured, of course," he adds. We hope he dropped Kim off on land somewhere along the coast. He's told the whole press corps that he had technical problems. Surely he dropped Kim off somewhere so her life wouldn't be at risk?

It's possible that he left her at the harbor in Køge, southwest of Amager. That's where the submarine sank, according to the first reports we received. But if that's what happened, why hasn't Kim called? Even if she lost her cell or if the battery was dead, she would have been in touch. There are phones everywhere, and she would have never let Ole or us worry needlessly. We ask if we can talk to the submarine man there in the back seat of the police car. He's the only one who knows where Kim is. Is she still on board? Another policeman denies our request, kindly but firmly. He tells us to go to the police station at Halmtorvet in the center of Copenhagen.

Should we drive to Køge and search on our own, or follow the policeman's instructions? We decide to follow the submarine man to the police station. She went out in the submarine with him yesterday evening, and now he's come back alone. Where did he leave her? I've lost count of how many times we've called her different phone numbers—she has Danish, Swedish, and American SIM cards. We've already clogged her Messenger account.

Those reassuring messages we sent earlier to family and friends are now followed by ones that are significantly more alarming: "Kim is still missing—we don't know where she is or what's happened."

The police station at Halmtorvet is near Istedgade, a Copenhagen street once notorious for drugs, crime, and prostitution. There are no parking spaces to be had, so we drive around the block several times. Finally, we take a spot outside the station, one designated for police cars. Just now, parking tickets seem like a minor concern.

We're met by a serious but friendly police officer and shown into a cold room on the ground floor. We wait, unsure exactly what we're waiting for. We hope it's a message that Kim's been found, unharmed, but such a message never arrives. Our phones are our lifeline to the outside world. We hear that the media crowd has moved from Dragør to Halmtorvet and that they're waiting outside the police station.

Ole is the first to be summoned to an interview in another part of the large building. Then we, too, are brought upstairs to what looks like the detectives' workroom. Personal belongings—a gym bag, used coffee cups—are our clues. The windows offer a view of gray roofs, and I realize we are quite high up in the building. We're offered coffee before the interview begins.

We're sitting in adjacent rooms, probably being asked the same detailed questions. My interviewer is a forty-something policewoman with a ponytail. I'm a little surprised to see that she and her colleagues all have pistols in their belts. In Sweden, officers with desk jobs wouldn't carry weapons. But I don't ask her about it.

She and I struggle our way forward in a mixture of Danish and Swedish, and I try to answer all her questions. The first one has to do with when I last had contact with Kim:

"Enjoy your trip to Berlin. See you Tuesday night. I love you! Kiss, kiss!" Kim said to me at lunchtime on Thursday. I'm out walking the dog in the lovely late summer sunshine when I call her. She's curious to hear what we think about Ole, whom we had just met the evening before. I joke and say that he gets high marks. And I add, "Keep this one."

"Don't worry—he's the one. So you'd better get used to having him around for the rest of our lives," she replied.

During the interview, each of us is asked to describe Kim's life, health, job, and future plans. We're asked to talk about her friends and her relationship with Ole. We tell them about Kim and Ole's decision to move to China and about our most recent meeting. We also have questions: What about her phone? Can they trace the most recent phone call? Where and when? We know she sent pictures to Ole just before the *Nautilus* was supposed to dive to the bottom of Öresund. What's happened since then?

What does the submarine man say? Where did he drop Kim off? We don't get any answers. But the policewoman interviewing me tells me Madsen is in custody. I'm very surprised. Why? The answer I get is that this is standard procedure, and something necessary in order to do a forensic examination of the man and guarantee his rights. My doubts start to grow. Too many hours have passed since Kim disappeared. She'd never stay away voluntarily. She wouldn't run away with someone else. She had no thoughts of suicide. On the contrary, her eyes were shining with happiness when we saw her the day before she disappeared. Ole is the love of her life, and she was looking forward to beginning that life together with him in earnest. If Kim's been injured, someone would have found her by now. We're in the middle of a densely populated area in one of Scandinavia's capital cities.

Tom makes the trip to Copenhagen from his work in Helsingborg. He's led into the police station without being discovered by the reporters. We're sitting together in the police break room to wait for the transcript of our interviews. They have to be corrected several times— Swedish and Danish aren't always compatible. The break room at Halmtorvet looks like many others—a large refrigerator, a sink, a coffeemaker. On the wall there's a bulletin board where the menu from a nearby pizzeria is posted next to what looks to me like shift schedules and information from the union. There are a few empty coffee cups on the rectangular table, salt and pepper shakers, a couple of newspapers, and the remote for the large TV that dominates one wall. While we're sitting here waiting for the final version of the interview transcripts, drinking yet another cup of vending-machine coffee, Tom turns on the TV. The submarine drama is the first story. All of a sudden, "breaking news" rolls past at the bottom of the screen: Peter Madsen has been arrested for murdering the Swedish journalist.

Time stands still. This can't be true. Kim is somewhere out there—we're just waiting for her to get in touch. The police officers who enter the room see the same thing we've just seen.

This is not how you're supposed to receive news of a loved one's death.

It's nobody's fault, but it feels like someone just pulled the carpet out from under my feet with a violent jerk. The television reports are about our daughter, our Kim: the woman who traveled all over the world, taking calculated risks when she had to, letting us know where she was every time she had access to Wi-Fi. Slowly, slowly the words sink in—the police believe she's been murdered on board the *Nautilus*. They are clearly affected by what's happened, upset over the way we've learned the news. In silence, they follow us out and make sure no reporters are waiting for us.

Our car is still there, untouched. We decide to drive to the outermost tip of Refshale Island, the place where Peter Madsen claimed he let Kim off on Thursday evening. It's dark and a little windy, and we find we're not alone—reporters are here for the same reason we are. We drive back and forth along the route Kim would have walked if Madsen had dropped her off. Could something have happened on her way to the apartment she shared with Ole? The flame of our last hope flickers brightly. We want so badly to wake up and find it was just a bad dream.

It's very late that evening when we get home to Gislöv Beach, on the southern coast of Scania, the southernmost province of Sweden.

We thought we would be away for five days. Instead, we're back home the same day. It hurts, both physically and psychologically. The only thing we've had all day is many cups of bad coffee—so many, we can't even count them. We turn on the TV—it's the same report that's on our phones, the radio, our computers.

The story of the female journalist who disappeared when covering a story on a homemade submarine in Copenhagen is repeated everywhere we look.

On TV, over and over, we see the image of Peter Madsen as he steps onto land. He stumbles off the boat deck and gives a thumbs-up to the journalists waiting in the harbor area. He looks carefree, not at all affected by what has happened to him: He's been rescued from the ocean after his submarine suddenly sank. So far, only a few people know that our family is the one hit by this enormous tragedy. This will soon change. On the other side of the Atlantic, news of Kim's disappearance has already started to spread. One of Kim's friends, Mustafa Hameed, works for CPJ—the Committee to Protect Journalists—and his colleagues in Europe have sounded the alarm for the missing journalist. At 11:43 p.m., Mustafa posts a message on a closed group on Facebook: It's Kim—she's the one who's disappeared. Immediately, people begin to react from all over the world; Kim has friends everywhere.

CHAPTER 3

"Or maybe I'll be a foreign correspondent. That would be fun." That's how Kim answered in 2011 when a local paper, *Trelleborgs Allehanda*, asked what she would be doing in five years. Kim is twenty-four years old and about to leave for the big wide world, for an internship at the Delegation of the European Union in New Delhi. She has a degree from the London School of Economics and Political Science under her belt. She's anxious to get going, to try her wings.

> *In five years I'll be working for an international organization. I would love to work in something related to diplomacy. Preferably with issues of development, aid, conflict resolution, and justice. Or maybe I'll be a foreign correspondent. That would be fun.*

The idea that the pen may be mightier than diplomacy is there, if still sleeping. Less than two years later—in 2013—Kim won first place in the Foreign Press Association's competition for young journalists.

She went to receive the prize a few weeks before she graduated from the School of Journalism at Columbia University in New York. It was a great honor, and quite a sum of money. This is how Kim explained her choice of profession in her acceptance speech:

Thank you so much. It's certainly an interesting time to become [a] journalist. My parents still struggle to understand my career choice. Because they're both journalists, too. My mother started working as a reporter at a local newspaper the day she graduated from high school. They used typewriters back then.

My father, who is a press photographer, started even earlier. When he was fifteen, he got on a moped with his first camera, and drove some fifteen miles to a beach resort where he had heard the Beatles were doing yoga. And he managed to get a picture of George Harrison, and sold it for the equivalent of five dollars. It was a very different era.

Both of my parents always worked full-time, so I spent a lot of my childhood in newsrooms. Or traveling. They always made sure to turn our family holidays into freelance pieces. Or vice versa, perhaps. When my classmates went to Greece or Italy, we crossed the Mexican border on a bus, or interviewed slave ancestors in the Caribbean. It wasn't really a conventional Swedish childhood.

But my parents definitely never intended to be my role models professionally. As the first person in my family with a university degree, they had high expectations for me. That I would do something that would pay well enough to support them when they retire. Or at least pay back a student loan. My younger brother has worked as a photojournalist for the past four years, so he's already a lost cause.

And it looked promising for a while—a year ago, I had just graduated with a degree in international affairs and had worked for the Swedish foreign ministry in Australia and for the European Union in India as a political reporter. But writing in diplomacy is very different from journalism. To me, it seemed contradictory—I was in some of the most exciting places in the world, and reporting on fascinating topics, but what I wrote was really quite bland. There are no scenes or characters in diplomatic writing. And the more important the topic, the smaller the readership. As we saw when WikiLeaks came out, there really are some great writers in diplomacy that people will—normally—never read . . .

So when I came here, I had no real journalistic experience to speak of. It was a steep learning curve, for sure. And now as I graduate, two weeks from today, there is a lot of pessimism toward and within the field. The Wall Street Journal just listed newspaper reporter as the worst job of 2013—two hundredth place out of two hundred, just below lumberjack. And foreign correspondence is perhaps especially difficult, as many news organizations have cut down their overseas bureaus for years now. But this is the paradox of journalism today, because people consume more news than ever before. And news coverage is far more global than it used to be . . . I don't think foreign correspondence is a dying business at all. It's just changing.

My dad kept saying . . . that good journalism was all about being in the right place at the right time. We often took detours when he picked me up from school to get some shots of a plane crash, or follow a car chase. And although so much has changed so quickly since then, one thing has remained constant. No matter the speed of technology and level of communication today—there is still no substitute for real reporting. Boston [referring to the bombing of the Boston Marathon] . . . is just one example of the problems poor reporting combined with social media can cause. If there's one thing I learned, it's that. Even today, there is no substitute for actually going there.

This is why the support of the Foreign Press Association means so much to me. In three weeks I will start an internship with the South China Morning Post in Hong Kong. I spent so much time in newsrooms as a kid, but this will be my first real experience as a professional journalist. And when foreign reporting has such an uncertain future, I am so glad that someone believes not just in me as a reporter, but also in what I hope to be doing for a living. I am really so honored to be here tonight. And my parents have—almost—stopped asking what my backup plan is, when journalism doesn't work out . . . [N]ow is a strange time to become [a] journalist, but I'm just so excited.

CHAPTER 4

Saturday, August 12, 2017

After a nearly sleepless night, we wake up to the worst Saturday of our lives. This morning we should have been enjoying breakfast at a hotel in Berlin. As we had so many times before, we would have strolled around Berlin, sat at an outdoor café, maybe enjoyed a boat ride on the Spree. Instead, we're trying to take in everything we experienced yesterday. It's been thirty-six hours since Kim boarded the submarine. What happened to her? Hope is slowly starting to disappear. If Kim is alive, why haven't we heard from her? Why are the Danish police calling her disappearance a murder?

Copenhagen's legal mills start grinding at 10:00 a.m. What we don't yet know, but will come to learn the hard way, is that Kim's name will be released in connection with this. It is only a few minutes past ten when media from both sides of Öresund call. What do we have to say? Nothing, absolutely nothing. We don't know anything except that Kim has disappeared without a trace. To satisfy the reporters' hunger, which becomes more and more insatiable—and which we know so well from our own work—we decide to write a short press release:

Kim Wall, Trelleborg

It is with great distress that we, her family, have received the news that Kim is missing after an assignment in Denmark. We believe, and earnestly hope, that she will be found safe and sound. Kim is 30 years old and educated at the Sorbonne in Paris, the London School of Economics in London, and Columbia University in New York, among other places. At Columbia, she received her Master's Degree in Journalism in 2013. Since then, she has worked all over the world and reported from such places as the Pacific Ocean, Africa, Asia, and the United States. She has home bases in New York and Beijing. Kim is strongly focused, ambitious, and devoted to her work. She often writes about social issues, foreign policy, pop culture, and issues of equality.

Our journalistic training kicks in. Now we are the professionals, reporters, who have dealt with cases like this many times before. However, there's a huge difference: This story involves our daughter and sister. We add a brief summary of Kim's CV and a photo Tom took a few years ago. During one of Kim's visits home, there was a brother-sister photo session at Tom's studio.

We look through the pictures we know that Kim likes. We choose a serious one. We want the world to have a suitable picture of Kim. We want the world to recognize that she disappeared while on assignment, that her work as a journalist took her to the place where she was last seen.

Saturday continues the same way it began. Our phones don't stop ringing, our email in-boxes ding constantly. The radio and television continue their reports, and Kim quickly becomes first-page news in many countries. Relatives and friends get in touch; the local paper's publication of Kim's name and picture means that all of Trelleborg soon knows what's happened. Work continues to pull the submarine out of Køge Bay. We follow the progress through media reports. We see the gray-black ship being raised up out of the water of the strait. What's it hiding? We don't let the dark thoughts penetrate to our consciousness, although they are pushing hard. At the same time, Peter Madsen stands before the judge in the courthouse in Copenhagen. Now it will be decided whether he'll be detained or not. We stay at home because we don't want to see the reporters crowding to get a seat in the courtroom. Nonetheless, it's through the work of the industrious reporters that we stay informed—they'll tell us minute by minute what's happening.

Peter Madsen wants to talk—he wants to tell what happened on board the *Nautilus*. The prosecutor and judge say no to an open courtroom, partly out of consideration for us. The hearing will therefore take place behind closed doors, and neither we, the press, nor any outside party will hear what Madsen says.

What does he want to say? Will he give an explanation of where Kim may be? Then the judge's decision comes: Madsen will be arrested. Not for homicide or manslaughter, but for something that in Sweden is called "causing another person's death"—involuntary manslaughter. A few days later, the phrase "grossly negligent" will be added to the charge—they said there had been an error in the record.

Late in the afternoon, the doorbell rings. This time it's not curious journalists, but rather two police officers, a man and a woman. This is the visit we've been anticipating with terror since yesterday evening, because it can mean only one thing: Kim is dead. We see in their body language that this is not an easy task for them. Bringing news of this kind must be something no human being gets used to. We sit down on the couches in the vestibule. After a brief silence, the policeman begins to speak. We receive the news we've been fearing.

Kim is gone forever. According to Madsen, she died when the heavy submarine hatch fell on her head as she was following him up the steps into the tower. He claimed that she died as a result of the blow, that he went into shock and went to bed to sleep for a few hours in the submarine at the bottom of Öresund. After waking up, he had decided to "bury" Kim at sea according to an old sailor tradition.

Now we can hear what was said in the courtroom a few hours earlier. Madsen admitted that Kim died on board under tragic circumstances. He didn't, however, answer the most obvious question: Why didn't he call for help? He was right outside one of the largest cities in Scandinavia, in the middle of significant maritime traffic—if you have an accident, don't you call for help? We're asked to keep the information to ourselves, and of course we do. We don't need to throw any more wood on the fire the media is stoking hour after hour. The submarine was recovered from the water under the eyes of a huge media audience. Soon there won't be one newspaper, radio station, TV channel, or online news source that's not reporting this drama. We won't be able to escape attention, and we see Kim's smiling face everywhere—on the TV screen, on our computers, in the newspapers.

The police need something that has Kim's DNA on it. Kim had left a toothbrush here and it's in my cup in the bathroom. The police put it carefully in a large bag. Ole is receiving the same dreadful message in Copenhagen. He provides Kim's hairbrush. Once the police have left, the tears finally come.

Now it's certain. We've received the worst news a parent can ever hear: Your child is gone. Your child has died. The tears flow and we hug each other, we cry into our dog Iso's warm fur. How horrible can life be? How unfair? Kim's life had just begun, and she had fought so hard—how on earth could it end like this?

And again, the questions: What happened? If it was an accident, why didn't Madsen call for help?

I wake up in the middle of the night. Two thoughts have taken shape in my mind during my uneasy slumber, two thoughts that stubbornly refuse to leave until I become conscious of them. One is that Kim will not be forgotten. She will live on through a scholarship fund. The other is that this book, the true story, must be written, and we are going to write it. Kim will be depicted as the involved, strong-willed woman she was, not as a victim. The decision gives me a bit of comfort—*a luta continua*—the fight continues.

Kim often saw life as just that, a fight that must be fought and that must be won. It didn't matter if it was a question of working her way into the male-dominated field of journalism, of writing the best articles, or of convincing the world to eat less meat. Kim lived according to her beliefs, and she seldom compromised.

Sunday, August 13, 2017

During the night, the submarine has been brought to land and set up in an industrial area in Nordhavnen, Copenhagen. The police investigation continues, but the submarine has to be emptied of over nine thousand gallons of water. The media are on-site.

We take a walk with Iso. Although our world has been turned upside down, our four-footed friend still needs walks along the beach. He understands that something's wrong, that his master and mistress are sad, and he tries to comfort us the way dogs do. He is unsuccessful. For the first time since Friday night, we forget to transfer our landline calls to our cell phones. We've been careful to do this every time we leave the house, because we don't want to miss any calls from the police. After a while, Jocke realizes that he's missed calls from a Danish number. He phones back—it's Jens Møller Jensen, head of the unit with the Copenhagen police that deals with crimes against persons. He's the one who is leading the investigation, and after just a couple of phone calls, we find we trust this calm Dane very much.

Jens wants to give us the news: Kim wasn't in the submarine. He's postponed his press conference in order to let us know first. This considerate act warms us in the middle of the maelstrom we're in, and we hurry home to follow the press conference. Jens Møller Jensen reports what we already know—or rather, don't know—about where Kim is. At the well-attended press conference in the yard outside the large police station, the police chief also reveals that the submarine seems to have been sunk intentionally. The crowd of reporters receives the news that the police are still looking for Kim, but that the hope of finding her alive is becoming smaller all the time. We know what Madsen said in the hearing, that Kim is dead, but we understand that the police don't want to announce this information yet.

Tips are streaming in to the police station in Copenhagen. Several people saw Kim when she stood in the tower of the submarine as it floated out from the harbor in Copenhagen in the late summer sun. But nobody seems to have seen Kim after eight thirty Thursday evening, either alive or dead. Kim is at the top of the news in much of the world: the *Washington Post*, the *New York Times*, the big German papers. There is an abundance of speculation, as is often the case when there aren't enough details. Why would you intentionally sink a submarine that you had made with your own hands? Something that you valued so highly? Would you sink it to hide a crime scene? The police's message to us—that Kim died accidentally—doesn't jibe with the sequence of events. So many questions, but one continues to gnaw at me: How is it possible that Madsen didn't ask for help?

Later the same day, we again cross the Öresund Bridge into Denmark, this time to pick up Kim's belongings. She and Ole were going to move to Beijing a few days later, and the apartment is basically already empty. Tom is with us, and his eye catches a half-transparent pen with Japanese characters on it. It's one of Kim's many Muji pens, the only ones she ever uses. In two months, the pen will play a starring role at the memorial ceremony at Columbia University in New York. A black suitcase with crooked wheels, a backpack, and a blue plastic IKEA bag—that's the sum of the worldly belongings Kim has left in Copenhagen.

Her laptop is lying idle in the same Chinese case we've seen so many times before. The silver Mac was her most important tool besides her phone and her Muji pens. It contained her life, her contacts with people all over the world, photographs, recordings of interviews, finished manuscripts, drafts, pitches, and chats.

Some of Kim and Ole's friends help us stow the things in our car. We cry and hug, but we don't say much—there aren't any words.

While we're in Copenhagen, the search mission continues in Køge Bay and Öresund. News of the search has been heard all over, and a lot of pleasure boats are helping to look. The orange sweater Ole told police Kim was wearing should help—it's riotously bright and easy to spot. At the same time, we know that if Kim is dead, it will be a number of days before her body reaches the surface.

There's nothing we can do. The Danish police are searching with airplanes and helicopters and have divers in the water. The examination of the submarine continues, and we receive news from Danish radio. Going to see the submarine is not an option: We don't want to see the vessel where our daughter probably lost her life, and the site is besieged by teams of reporters.

At home in Trelleborg, we sit down and try again to make sense of it all. We can't. We don't know what happened, and we can't imagine how what seemed to be such a simple gig could go so wrong.

Many journalists have already written about Madsen. Several had been out on the submarine. What happened to Kim? As usual, she was very well prepared, and a while ago she had interviewed Madsen's previous friends and companions, now enemies, from the space race. People we know and people we don't know contact us—Kim's disappearance has moved and engaged them. We simply can't talk, don't want to tell the story—we don't know anything. We make do with a brief status update on Facebook, the channel that at times relays information better than the media:

> *Thank you so much for all your support, all your hugs and warmth, that we're getting during these days, the worst ones of our lives. It feels good to know that despite everything, there's still so much good in the world.*

It doesn't take long before 321 people have read it and shown their empathy. These people are probably following the same media coverage we are. The TV channels are showing a smiling Kim standing in the submarine tower, on her way through the harbor outlet in Copenhagen. She looks happy—she's going to write a story about a man who has devoted his life to submarines and space rockets. She's sure that she'll be able to sell the story, and she can have the experience of diving to the bottom of Öresund. She'll have one more exciting story to tell for years to come.

CHAPTER 5

March 1987

It was a gray, chilly Monday at the end of March. The wind was blowing, and as is common in southern Scania, we had horizontal rain—today mixed with snowflakes. Only a couple of days earlier, on Saturday, we had sat outside in the garden for the first outdoor coffee of the year. The sun was shining, giving hope of spring around the corner. I was very pregnant. The baby, whose working name was Sigge, was supposed to have arrived on Friday. The father-to-be had been off work the whole week, the bag was packed, and the dog sitter ready to spring into action. Now it was Monday, another workday. Jocke had driven into Malmö to his job as a press photographer with *Kvällsposten*. He had only been gone a few hours before I noticed something was starting to happen. A quick phone call to Malmö, and then we were on our way to the maternity ward in Trelleborg. Just after nine thirty that evening, our daughter came into this world—so longed for, and already so loved.

She got her nickname there in the maternity ward, a nickname that would stick with her well into her school years. To Grandmother Lilly, it was our daughter's name for the rest of her life.

Officially, Kim was Kim, but among family and friends, she was Mumlan. The name came from the way she would burrow into her blanket. At least that's how we interpreted it. In Jocke's native language, German, the concept is known as *einmummeln*, and in Swedish *mumla in sig*. Mumlan was a child who was easy to love. She was alert, curious, happy, and incredibly social, even in her first weeks. In the evenings, she had no intention of sleeping in her beautiful cradle. She wanted to spend time together with her mother, eating constantly.

In the summer of 1988, we took a three-week trip through Europe. Sometimes we slept in our old yellow four-person tent; other times we treated ourselves to a hotel or, as we did in Hungary, to a worn-down hostel. Traveling as parents, we had a bit more to do. Mumlan was a very mobile child. She was always curious, and so her life was one big exploration. She didn't want to miss anything—everything had to be examined. The doves on the Stephansplatz in Vienna had to be chased—it was so much fun for her to have them flying around her little legs, the little girl in a pink-striped Minnie Mouse dress and white sandals. That summer, we also knew that our family would soon have four members instead of three. Child number two was arriving at the end of the year, and Mumlan was going to be a big sister. In our world, having children didn't mean you couldn't travel anymore. In the summertime, we started with a tent and then moved on to a camper, which we drove through Europe. In the winter, our trips took us across the Atlantic—to Florida, California, and Mexico.

The trip to Mexico, however, was a little more adventurous than we had anticipated. We flew from Kastrup Airport in Copenhagen to Los Angeles, and from there took a bus to Baja California, a trip that would take "just a few hours." Since we'd been in the US several times with the children, we thought a sun-and-surf vacation in Mexico would be fun. But when we landed in Los Angeles, it was way too late for the just-a-few-hours trip over the border. The next day, we learned that the few hours meant twelve, and that our bus didn't have any air-conditioning to speak of. Once again, our children showed us what strong personalities they had even as two- and three-year-olds. No complaining—just many, many stories.

Once in Baja California, again late at night, our hotel smelled like mold, the temperature was below fifty degrees, and it wasn't just "off season"—it was completely abandoned. The village slept, and you couldn't swim or sunbathe. We packed our bags, put the children in their twin stroller, and found the local bus station. We drew some attention with our two red suitcases and a stroller full of children and backpacks.

However, in very deficient Spanish, we were able to book tickets to the US border. After several hours riding through a barren desert, we arrived. Now we would cross the border on foot. We must have been some of the strangest-looking people the border police and the customs officials had ever seen. They searched through our bags very thoroughly and poked needles into the children's stuffed animals, to their great despair.

They probably suspected us of smuggling heroin. We weren't, of course—we were just trying to salvage our vacation.

In the middle of the night, our Greyhound bus arrived at the downtown station in San Diego—not exactly a good place for a family with two children. We ended up taking a taxi to the airport, where we thought there had to be a rental car. To our relief, there was. Now our vacation could begin in earnest.

It turned out to be the right decision, and during those weeks we got to see Tijuana, San Diego, Disneyland, and much more. It ended up being a great vacation after all. And all four of us learned a lot. You really can travel with children.

During the spring of 1990, while we waited for a day care opening, I worked half-time. Our parental leave was over, and there was no day care to be had. The children would follow me out on assignments whenever possible, so I had time to take care of my job on those days that Jocke was working at his. An understanding employer as well as Grandmother's and Grandfather's flexible working hours meant that there were never, or at least seldom, any problems. Although eventually it became natural for the children to come with us to work, in the beginning—in the spring of 1988—when Jocke took paternal leave with Kim, it was still a rather new phenomenon. It was even more unusual for a photographer who had union duties and had the nerve to bring his babbling daughter with him to meetings and negotiations. There's no doubt that at least one or two people didn't like it, but for us there was no alternative.

While she was growing up, Kim spent a lot of time at editors' desks and in newspaper environments. The idea of a child's perspective wasn't yet invented, but for us it was a reality. If you're going to write about children's theater, shouldn't you be able to see the production through a child's eyes?

Kim's character became more obvious during her years at Dalajär Preschool. She had no problem keeping herself occupied—she was incredibly creative and inspired the other students. She wasn't the focus of the class—rather the opposite. This was probably because she was a bit older than many of the children and was entering a group that was already established. She took responsibility for Tom, who quickly learned that his big sister functioned as a spokesperson for him. I think the part of the day she enjoyed most was when all the other children had left and she got to settle into her teacher's lap to listen to a story. Books and storytelling became a large part of Kim's life very early on. We read a lot at home—no evening went by without at least one story! There were favorites, the ones Kim could recite better than Mamma or Pappa. *Baby Kalle's Birthday* was a book we sometimes wished we could hide somewhere. Mamma Mu, Pettsson and Findus, Emil—these were the classic Swedish favorites that were read again and again.

Even as a small child, Kim solved any problem that got in her way. Her creativity and imagination were vast, and nothing was impossible.

I think she was about four when her interest in dinosaurs took off. Soon she knew everything about these prehistoric creatures, and the hard-to-pronounce names were no match for her. She built settings for her small dinos and created entire worlds for them. Of course, we didn't think they were particularly appealing.

Her dinosaur period lasted quite a while, and it was certainly no coincidence that the first book Kim read entirely on her own was *The Land Before Time*, which features giant lizards. She always thought that our bedtime stories were too short and too few, and to solve this problem, she learned to read on her own. When she stumbled over a difficult word, she asked for help. If she couldn't find a word, she invented one. She might have been two years old when, fascinated by convertibles, she stated that there were cars in Florida "without lids." She thought the word *duvet* was strange; it ought to be called "blanket case." She quickly baptized our trailer Kulingen—it was so "cool" (*kul*) to travel around Europe in it—and that name has stuck to this day. The bike carrier on our car became the "bike grabber," and that is, of course, exactly what it is.

From childhood and into adulthood, nature and its care interested Kim deeply. As parents, we listened many times as Kim lectured us about unnecessary car trips and wasted food. The need to have empathy for the underdog, for those without a voice, was absolutely obvious to her from early on.

Kim was never afraid of speaking up when she thought something was wrong. When Kim and her friend Elina heard that the big, beautiful copper beech tree in the kindergarten playground was going to be cut down because it was considered a danger to the children, they became tree huggers despite their tender age. The girls wrote petitions and created a poster that was put on the trunk of the beech. Nobody was going to cut down their beloved tree! With uneven letters, they printed their message and encouraged others to stand up for their tree. They were successful, and the tree was examined once again. It was found to be healthy, and it's still standing.

I don't know what Kim learned from this experience. When we talked about it a few years ago, she didn't even remember this episode. But she fought for what she felt was right, and we got to see this ability in her many times. If something's wrong, you have to speak up. The culture of silence was not her way.

CHAPTER 6

Monday, August 14–Saturday, August 19, 2017

Our home has been transformed into a florist's shop. Several times a day, a delivery arrives with the most beautiful bouquets. We run out of vases, and then out of glass jars, and then we have nothing left to put them in. Close friends, work colleagues, more remote acquaintances, people from our past—their warmth thaws our frozen hearts. One of the florist's shops does some quick thinking and brings us a load of vases we can borrow—one of the many acts of thoughtfulness that do us good. Phone calls, emails, letters, and cards—we receive more assurances of how Kim's fate has moved so many more than we can count. Her friends get in touch from all the world's corners. They send pictures and share memories from their time together with Kim. We alternate between laughing and crying. Our feelings run in all directions—a word, a picture, anything at all can bring the tears again.

Soon a private group is formed on Facebook—"Friends and Family of Kim Wall." Here our memories are collected. Many of them make us laugh. The pictures of when she and her friends in London had fun sliding down a dorm staircase on a mattress make for a cheery hour.

It's so like Kim—she has to have been the one behind this mischief. Despite her age and her impressive academic training, her playfulness was never far beneath the surface. Kim knew how to make the sun shine in an environment that, to a large extent, consisted of dogged study.

May Jeong, a colleague and close friend of Kim's, posts a message on Facebook about Kim's disappearance and encourages everyone to get in touch with us with pictures and memories. She also posts a picture of Kim, taken on Christmas Day 2016. This is what May writes:

> *Kim's about to crack open a coconut. We've just come back from Arugam Bay, covered with mosquito bites but happy. We know we're young and full of dreams. I remember I wrote those words in my diary—young and full of dreams.*

A couple of days later, through a staticky Skype line, May tells us the background of the cracked coconuts. She and Kim had heard from the locals that at the end of the year, you're supposed to break open coconuts while wishing to be rid of something in your life along with the year that's about to turn. The friends couldn't possibly resist such a challenge. May and Kim agreed on two things they wished out of their lives—the patriarchy and bad editors who don't keep their promises.

For us, the days must go on despite everything.

We get up every morning, take a shower, walk the dog. But nothing feels real. Friends get in touch, and people bring us meals. They offer to walk Iso and want to make our everyday lives as easy as possible. So much love, and so much warmth. We hug each other and we try to comfort each other. This is bottomless despair. No parents should have to experience this. The truth is merciless. Illness, accident, terrorism—if

Kim had been taken from us by any of these, our grief would have been just as great, but maybe easier to accept. To die in a submarine in Copenhagen, forty-five minutes from her parents' house—such things don't happen. Or so we thought. We think a lot about the explanation the policeman gave us—that Kim was hit in the head by the heavy submarine hatch and died of her injuries. Can that really be true? Our minds grind away, day and night.

At the same time, we're besieged. Outside on our little residential street, there are Danish and German cars. When we go out to get the paper and mail from our mailbox, we're asked if we want to say something. We don't. Reporters ring our doorbell and receive the same answer. They pay visits to our neighbors and contact our relatives and acquaintances. Very few have anything to say. We're all in a state of shock, and we hope we'll soon wake up from this nightmare.

Danish TV 2 calls—the submarine story takes up all the airtime of a program that's their equivalent of *America's Most Wanted*. Do we want to work with them? We don't, but when Jens Møller Jensen tells us it can facilitate the search if witnesses come forth, we create a written release:

> We—Kim Wall's parents and brother—are experiencing the worst days of our lives. No one can imagine what we are going through. Kim has worked in many dangerous places in her work as a journalist, and there have been many times we've worried about her. That something could have happened in Copenhagen, just a stone's throw from her childhood home, is something we could never have imagined. Now it looks as though the worst has happened. That is why we—Ingrid, Joachim, and Tom Wall—appeal to any of you who might be able to help us find out what has happened. We have great confidence in the way the police are working, and we hope passionately that the public will contribute with information

*that can help them solve the case. Please contact the police in
Copenhagen or Malmö and tell them anything you know. We
can't imagine anything better than getting our Kim back safe
and sound, but we realize that the chances are very small.
Even so, please let us know what has happened.*

—Ingrid, Joachim, and Tom Wall, Trelleborg, August 17,
2017

On the other side of the Atlantic, different organizations are
involved in expressing the importance of a continued rigorous search.
The CPJ issues a statement.

So does IWMF, the International Women's Media Foundation.
They sharply urge the Danish police to do everything to find Kim.
Kim's personal friends are behind the message, friends who work to
improve the conditions of journalists in a world that is becoming more
and more hostile to the fourth estate. The news of her disappearance has
stirred up strong feelings. One of her Swedish friends, Malin Franzén,
says in a TV interview: "Kim is a smart woman. She's both academically
smart and street wise. It would be strange if someone got the better of
her." The words make us once again dwell on what might have happened on board. The theory of an accident makes it easier to bear, in
a way. An accident can't be predicted; it's no one's fault. But if it was
an accident, why didn't Madsen call for help? Why did he take it upon
himself to "bury" Kim?

In the spring of 2016, Kim went through HEFAT, Hostile Environment
and First Aid Training, which lasted several days. The course was part of
the preparations for a trip to Uganda. Together with a group of other
female journalists, she was trained in self-defense, how to behave during
a hostage situation, and much more. Kim was glad and thankful for the

training in Kenya, and she was very aware of the dangers she was expos-ing herself to during her travels, particularly in the developing world.

The summer before, we had gone through the test questions and answers that might be used in a kidnapping situation.

Kim was in no way a wide-eyed innocent, and she had followed colleagues' fates in Syria and Africa. We decided on a number of ques-tions that only she and her closest family circle knew the answers to. For us, it seemed rather strange, but Kim insisted, "so you know what you're supposed to tell the kidnappers if it happens." We decided on the trailer's nickname and the type of tree that grows outside her window. Kim knew she could get into trouble, and she wanted us to be prepared. I don't think she was afraid that something was going to happen, but she was realistic enough to know that the world can be a dangerous place. She had been mugged in both Cuba and Sri Lanka, and several of her colleagues had been attacked and roughed up.

For several weeks, the search for Kim continues with undiminished strength. Every day that goes by means that our hope withers more, until it finally dies altogether. Now we just want them to find Kim's remains. Every walk along the beach is a search for flotsam. We hear helicopters searching for Kim, and we know that ships all over the region are doing the same. They should be able to see her glaring orange sweater, shouldn't they?

We live quite near the shore of the Baltic Sea and take Iso down to the beach several times a day. The waves have always had a calming effect on me. When I've had a stressful day at work with a lot of prob-lems to solve, everything seems better when I walk along the Baltic.

But now it feels different. That ocean out there holds our Kim.

We jump every time the phone rings. The adrenaline rushes through our bodies, and our pulses increase—are we finally going to find out? It doesn't happen. Nobody has any answers for us. The search continues on both sides of Öresund. Volunteers work side by side with the authorities. The sea rescue forces send their members—there is a strong desire to find Kim and let us have closure. This is the worst feeling of all—not knowing.

I drive in to the Central Station in Trelleborg to meet Ole, who's coming by train from Copenhagen. I stand on the platform, completely unaware that everyone around me knows by this time what's happened. People I know and people I don't know look my way, and many hug me. The tears stream down while others rush by with a quick glance in my direction. This is the first time, but nowhere near the last, that I experience a fame that I would give anything to be without.

On Saturday, some of Kim's friends visit us. They come from New York, Dubai, Oslo, and Copenhagen. We're overwhelmed by their decision to drop everything, jump on a plane, and come to see us. Several of them we've never met before. We've heard about their adventures with Kim, but we've never met in real life until now. Suddenly, the house is full of young people. Laughter mixes with tears; happy memories chase away our grief for a few hours.

Kim had a very full life. What amazing friends she's had. It ends up being a comforting day after all. Mansi Choksi brings a small framed picture of the Indian god Ganesha for us. During a trip that Kim and Mansi took to Sri Lanka, Kim talked about how she had learned to swim on Bali, in a swimming pool where a statue of Ganesha sprayed water. She was seven years old then, but the memories from all the trips she had taken with us had left deep imprints on her mind. Sadef Ali Kully has brought Kim's favorite biscuits and marmalade. We talk about Kim's weakness for karaoke. We laugh about the time when the Christmas turkey got charred and the poor cook landed in the emergency room with second-degree burns. We cry about our loss, about Kim, who had left so many things undone—we cry as we think about all the impressions she's made on people all over the world. We float the idea of a fund in Kim's name. The response is immediate—what a great idea! Of course we'll do it. Mansi and Sadef volunteer to ask the IWMF if they will be the sponsor.

This evening it feels easier to breathe, despite everything. We're not alone in our grief. We now have a new family, spread out all over the world. We're united in one thing—our love for Kim and everything she gave us. And everything we've lost.

Who is this person Kim sailed out into Öresund with? The man who, in one way or another, kept Kim from coming back to us—who is he?

During this past week, Peter Madsen and the submarine story have dominated the news. Gradually, the picture of an eccentric person takes shape. Madsen was born in 1971, the youngest of four brothers. They all have the same mother, but different fathers. When his parents divorce, Peter, who's now six, gets to choose with whom he wants to live. He chooses his father, who is considerably older than his mother. This man has a great interest in space and space exploration. According to the reports, Wernher von Braun, the Nazi-German rocket engineer called "the conqueror of space," is one of his father's idols. Media reports claim that this impressed young Peter, who shows an early interest in space and rockets. While he's still a teenager, his father dies. The boy attempts several different majors without ever graduating. His ambition is to be an engineer, but he never finishes his studies. He takes courses in welding and becomes good at it. Peter Madsen's great interest in rockets means that he is considered something of a nerd. At fifteen, in 1986, he sends his first homemade rocket up in a yard near his home. The rocket is about three feet tall, and he christens the launch area Cape Cosmos.

Eventually, Madsen's interest in space expands to include submarines. In 2002, he builds his first submarine, which he calls *Freya*. A few years later, it's followed by submarine number two, *Kraka*. In 2008, *Nautilus* is finished, and at that time it was the world's largest homemade submarine. It's launched with much pomp and circumstance in the harbor in Copenhagen.

Together with others who share his interest in rockets and space exploration, Peter Madsen becomes involved in Copenhagen Suborbitals, an association of people whose goal is to send a manned rocket to space and back. Many people are curious and wander over to Refshale Island and the abandoned wharf buildings to see the experiment. Around a thousand people also support the project financially. In 2014, however, Madsen has a difference of opinion with the other members of Copenhagen Suborbitals and leaves the group. In the neighboring building, an old workshop, he establishes his own company, RML, which stands for Rocket Madsen Space Lab. Here he continues to build on his dream to reach space. A launch of the rocket *Flight Alpha* is planned for August 26 and 27, 2017. This is going to happen off the shore of Bornholm, the Danish island off the southern coast of Sweden, and the plan is that Madsen and a few like-minded friends will sail there on the *Nautilus* on August 11. The day before Kim goes on board the submarine, Peter Madsen cancels the trip. The general picture that takes shape from the news reports is of a strongly driven person who wants to execute his plans no matter what. He surrounds himself with other people who share his passion for space exploration. His finances are meager, and at times Madsen lives in the workshop or the submarine to save money. He has never actually held down a real job.

CHAPTER 7

November 2009

All summer and fall of 1989, the news reports followed the sequence of events in countries behind the Iron Curtain. In Leipzig there were demonstrations—many had escaped to Hungary to make their way over to the West. By coincidence, the whole Wall family was in Germany when the Berlin Wall fell in November 1989. Tom was ten months old, Kim was two and a half years old. We had neglected to book a hotel room—we knew that it was still well ahead of the Christmas market season, so there was sure to be something. But we were wrong. There was a huge convention in Hamburg, so we struck out at hotel after hotel. Finally, we ended up a good distance from the center of town, in Pinneberg. Jocke went inside to see if they had room for us while I waited in the car with the children. When he came back out, he said he had heard on the television in the reception area that the Wall had fallen. Fallen! Was it possible? We settled into a room at the top of the building. Jocke wanted more than anything to get back into the car and drive to Berlin to take photographs and experience the historic event.

I protested—I didn't want to be left alone with two small children, and, given the chaos we saw on TV, it could take days to get there and back.

The next day, we experienced the Reunification in Lübeck. The old city's streets were full of East German Trabis, the communist country's answer to the VW Beetle. The West Germans put candy and flowers under their windshield wipers. We wandered the historic streets at the same time history was being written.

Kim has, of course, heard a lot about this during her childhood. She heard about the brutal regime behind the Iron Curtain, about the Fall of the Wall and the new, beautiful world she's been privileged to grow up in. A world without war, a world where liberty, fraternity, and equality reign. In theory, anyway.

In 2009, twenty years have passed since the Fall of the Berlin Wall. We decide early in the year that we want to be at the Brandenburg Gate on this anniversary. Jocke, Tom, and I drive to Berlin, and Kim arrives by plane from London. We meet her at a classic site, Bahnhof Berlin Friedrichstrasse, and we get to spend some lovely days in the German capital. As we've done so many times before, we rent an apartment in the neighborhood behind the Brandenburg Gate, next to the Holocaust Memorial and Hotel Adlon, with the American embassy across the street. We make a game of watching the big black limousines as they drive up to the entrance of the hotel. Suddenly, Hillary Clinton steps out of one car, and once again, we feel the wings of history. On the evening of November 9, there are tens of thousands of people who gather in front of the gigantic stage at the Brandenburg Gate.

Here, the most powerful people in the world will speak, either live onstage or, as Barack Obama does, through a video link. Kim succeeds—of course—in pushing her way to the front. She doesn't want to miss one word of what the powerful men and women say. This is what she wants to work with—this is her world. Now, almost ten years later, we find on her computer an unpublished article she wrote about the experiences in Berlin that cold, gray evening in November:

> *When I arrive at the Brandenburg Gate, it seems like most of the expected visitors, several hundred thousand, are already here. I'm pulled into a group only about 50 meters from the stage where the Berlin Wall stood two decades before, just a few minutes before the celebration of the anniversary is to begin. I'm already soaked through from the autumn rain falling, but two Frenchmen hold an umbrella over my head. Right in front of me there are barricades and policemen, there to block the way to the stage. For reasons of safety, they don't want to let people into this area, something that seems ridiculous given the large, empty space between us and the stage. After all, this is not a day one should be building walls. Happily chanting the slogan from 1989—"Wir sind ein Volk," we are one people—the comrades around me break down the provisional fence, and their running feet are accompanied by laughter. It all happens in the blink of an eye and the police can hardly object. As I run with them in what one could consider my first act of civil disobedience, I get a feeling that something similar happened the same night exactly 20 years ago—just on a much larger scale.*

> *Somehow I make my way to the Brandenburg Gate, where the speakers line up after the Berlin Philharmonic has performed. Hillary Clinton, Angela Merkel, Gordon Brown, Dmitry Medvedev, Nicolas Sarkozy, Lech Walesa. All of them here, except Obama, who instead sends his congratulations through a direct-broadcast speech from the White House, projected on gigantic TV screens. The air is full of mist from the rain and*

the excitement. Being here feels something like standing right under the stage at a rock concert, only much more intense. The most significant speaker is maybe Mikhail Gorbachev— the Soviet leader who in 1987 was directly encouraged by Reagan to "tear down this wall" and who was responsible for introducing glasnost, a necessary step towards the fall of the Iron Curtain. Behind me, 1,000 unique human-sized domino bricks are placed in a line, all decorated by children, artists and poets from all over the world. They form a symbolic wall, and they reach from the Potsdamer Platz past the Brandenburg Gate and up to the Reichstag.

The final speaker is José Manuel Barroso, President of the European Commission, who has the honor of toppling the first domino brick. When they fall, one by one, there are few eyes that are still dry. The cries of "Hurrah!" from thousands of people are accompanied by fireworks.

The American girls at my left ask me to take their picture in front of the Brandenburg Gate while Hillary Clinton is speaking.

Meanwhile, the Frenchmen to my right hug each other and ask me if I want to share their cigar—Pour la liberté! Around me I can see African and Asian people next to many Germans, each with his or her own story to tell about the Wall. We all truly have good reason to celebrate the 20th anniversary of the Fall of the Berlin Wall. Has a human structure ever had such a symbolic significance before? The Wall didn't just divide a city, a nation and its people, but signaled an ever-growing gap between east and west. When it fell, the Iron Curtain was— and is still—a victory for people all over the globe. It represents basic human rights, democracy and the immediate need for a grass-roots revolution. The Fall of the Wall was caused more by people than by political decisions. These values, important for us all, are even more important for those who are still closed behind barricades in other parts of the world. The "Great Firewall" in China which censors the Internet, the 2,500-mile barrier between India and Bangladesh that runs through villages and even through houses, and, most notably—our generation's Berlin Wall—the Israeli barricade on the West Bank: All of these still exist today. These physical and psychological walls, just as many others, will appear less and less justifiable in light of what happened during this weekend's festivities.

Maybe the large sums of money spent on this Fest der Freiheit—festival of freedom—are the most wisely used this side of the recession. Everything that can harass and force these decision-makers into a new era of glasnost by showing the absurdity of this antiquated model of artificial partitioning has to cost money.

By coincidence, I was actually here in Germany 20 years ago. I wasn't in Berlin, so I missed the sight of family, friends and lovers who fell into each other's arms, and soldiers who laid down their Kalashnikovs to open champagne bottles together with the jubilant masses. Since I was only two and one-half, I don't remember anything of what I actually saw—a massive stream of East Germans who came over to the west to enjoy their newly won freedoms. This included getting to wear clothes in colors other than gray, brown and blue, and to eat bananas every day. Individual freedom can only find space in such small things like these. After having witnessed and shared the uninhibited joy on November 9, 1989, I'm not sure I can experience this feeling, although two decades have passed. It's probably too much for a young person like me, born and raised in Sweden, a land with one of the planet's longest traditions of democracy, to understand.

The most crucial thing in recognizing historic events such as this is allegorical. By celebrating 20 years of a unified Germany, we can put the Iron Curtain into a context.

In addition, it's a perfect opportunity to recognize the situation of people who live segregated and oppressed in other places. This, rather than celebrating the historic turning point, is why the world's leaders are here today. It is for the individuals who live behind these remaining walls that these festivities are so significant. The Berlin Wall is fundamentally a metaphor that tells us that it is possible and necessary to tear down walls for people who are less fortunate than the citizens of Berlin.

—Kim Wall, November 2009, twenty-two years old

CHAPTER 8

Monday, August 21, 2017

I've decided to return to my job as head of information for the municipality of Trelleborg. In the midst of all that's been happening, everyday tasks feel comforting. Even if it's just a few moments when I succeed in thinking about something else, it's like a thread of normalcy to hold on to.

It's something of a soft start. A long time ago, this day was set aside as a planning retreat for security work that the municipality is conducting together with the police in Trelleborg and Söderslätt. We're a small group of six people who gather at Smygehus Havsbad, a picturesque old hotel near the sea. The warmth I feel from my colleagues is overwhelming, as are the hugs I get. Even the police officers with many years of experience with the dark side of life seem very affected by Kim's fate.

I can do this, I think. We're sitting in a room on the second floor, and by coincidence, I've chosen a seat facing the ocean. One window is open to let in the late summer breeze. They're still looking out there—the ocean is huge.

All of a sudden I see something orange a bit offshore. It's not moving—can it be? No, I don't think so. My heart skips a beat, and I try to focus on the glaring object in the big field of blue. I don't want to say anything, and after a while I realize that it's an orange buoy anchored out there.

We've been forewarned that today the police will make public what Peter Madsen said during his detention hearing nine days before—that Kim had died when the heavy submarine hatch struck her on the head, and that he had "buried" her afterward in Køge Bay.

We're sitting and discussing safety at Trelleborg's Central Station, when my telephone and tablet screen nearly explode. The police in Copenhagen have released the information, and the media's interest has quickly jumped into the red zone. The phone rings, and I get texts and tons of email. The press release from the police has created a new tsunami of articles.

It feels pretty good to force myself to concentrate on everyday matters such as safety walks, the social contract, and neighborhood cooperation.

I drive home slowly along the beautiful coast road from the southernmost peninsula in Scandinavia to Gislöv Beach, knowing that the information we have had for more than a week is now public. My first day at work has gone well—despite everything. *Now it can only get better,* I think.

I am so wrong.

Once home, I find out that the police in Copenhagen have sent out a new press release. A cyclist has found a corpse on the southern shore of Amager, the large island where Kastrup Airport is located. A while later, at 5:23 p.m., Jens Møller Jensen calls. He's on his way out to the site. Jens apologizes for giving us the news in this way, but he's eager to make sure that we get to hear it from him and not from the media. The Swedish sea rescue forces have been assisting their Danish colleagues today, and the media has been observing the search, both from the air with helicopters and at sea from boats. Many police officers in one place will always attract the media, says Jens, who doesn't think the find can be kept secret very long. He hopes he can have a few hours of undisturbed work, but his experience tells him this isn't going to happen. He has a grim message for us.

"It's a corpse without clothes, a corpse that has been destroyed in a way that I don't think would have happened if it had simply lain in the water. It has no arms. We don't know if it's Kim, but I think it is," says Jens. He adds that the police in Denmark have no other missing women it could possibly be.

The next few hours are uneasy as we follow the developments on TV. The pictures shown are macabre: a large white sheet lying on the black asphalt bike path. Divers and police are working along the shore and in the water. There are large stones that protect the path from winter storms, stones that now make it tricky to get down to the edge of the water.

Is that Kim lying under the sheet? Our beautiful, gifted daughter? We are torn between wishing it's true and hoping it isn't.

In the evening, Jens calls again. By now we recognize his number on the display. Jocke takes the call, and I sit next to him. "Oh no," says Jocke. Not just once, but several times. He turns pale.

When he hangs up, he turns to me and says, "Jens said that it's only a torso they found. No arms, no legs, no head."

The world stops.

Time stands still.

Tuesday, August 22, 2017

On Monday, we didn't think it could get any worse. It could. On Tuesday, we and the rest of the world learn that the arms, legs, and head were removed intentionally. It's not an accident—it's a conscious act by a human being. In addition, the body has been stabbed several times to keep it from floating up to the surface. For the same reason, a strap with weights has been wrapped around the body. Someone has gone to great lengths to make sure the body will stay on the bottom of the ocean.

The last tiny flicker of hope is still sputtering—maybe it's not Kim after all. We cling to this thought, although our senses tell us that it is.

The forensic experts are working hard. The toothbrush and hairbrush will give the answer—is there a DNA match between the body found at Amager and our daughter?

Wednesday, August 23, 2017

At 2:05 in the morning, the phone rings. It's Jens, who gives us the news that there is no longer any doubt. It's Kim's mutilated body the cyclist found at Amager on Monday afternoon.

A few hours later, Jens Møller Jensen, dressed in a black shirt and black jacket, stands in front of a crowd of journalists and announces the unthinkable—it is our daughter who is dead and violated.

"I want to express my deepest sympathies to the family of Kim Wall. Last night I had to give them the definitive news that a DNA match was made between Ms. Wall and the corpse that was found. This match, of course, signifies a relatively large breakthrough in the investigation, which will now continue," Jens says as he begins the press conference.

He talks about metal pieces, knife wounds, and the continued search for body parts and clothes. He talks about blood found on board the submarine. He appeals to the public to report anything they've seen that may have significance. Now it is final: Kim died on board this homebuilt vessel that isn't even a submarine at all.

Science has given us the answer we dreaded.

We can't meet the world, nor do we have the strength. But in order to accommodate the need for a reaction from us in some way, we post another statement on Facebook:

> It was with boundless sorrow and shock that we received the news that the remains of our daughter and sister Kim Wall have been found. We can't yet fathom the breadth of this catastrophe, and there are so very many questions that remain to be answered.
>
> This tragedy has not only affected us and the rest of our family, but also friends and colleagues all over the world. During the horrific days that have passed since Kim disappeared, we have received countless signs of how loved and appreciated she was, both as a human and as a professional journalist. Proof has arrived from all corners of the world of Kim's ability to be someone who makes a difference.
>
> She found and told stories from different parts of the globe, stories that simply had to be written. Kim traveled for several months in the Southern Pacific to let the world know what is happening to the people on the islands that are sinking as a result of atomic weapon detonation. She let us follow along to Haiti after its devastating earthquake, to Idi Amin's torture

chambers in Uganda, and to the minefields in Sri Lanka. She gave the weak, the vulnerable, the marginalized a voice. This voice, which we [should have been able to] hear for many years to come, is now silent.

I've worked with words my entire professional life—for more than forty years. These lines were among the hardest I have ever written. It meant that everything was irrevocable—Kim is dead, gone forever. Not away on an assignment, not out of Wi-Fi range, but simply, truly gone.

On Facebook, the condolences stream in, from people we know and from complete strangers. Kim's fate touches people. The television reporter Anja Kontor writes this:

> *KIM . . . Grief floods me. Kim . . . As a fellow human being, I can't stop thinking about you. Your family. The truth is so brutal. So repulsive. Every day at the seashore I've thought about you in that little chamber. You thought you were doing an interview in a submarine. Now your toothbrush has helped to identify your torso. (This thought makes me hurt all over physically to write.) I'm thinking about that little toothbrush. And about the violence against women that has once again snuffed out a life. Kim. Kim. May you have restitution! You who gave a voice to the weak all over the world.*

I go into Kim's room, the same room she's had since she was around one year old. The bags from Copenhagen are standing in the same spot where we put them that terrible Sunday after we came home. We simply can't unpack them, and why should we? What should we do with her belongings? The most important one, the laptop—we're very careful with that. The rest are simply earthly things.

On this dreadful day, we realize that internet trolls won't allow even a tragedy like this to pass without comment. One journalist on TV interpreted the press conference in Copenhagen while it was being broadcast live and happened to say that the toothbrush and hairbrush that had provided the DNA match were found in the submarine. New, wild speculations. Had she brought the toothbrush along in case she wanted to spend the night? And did she have other plans as well? We reacted quickly and contacted those responsible at the TV station, who immediately withdrew the comments. A wild theory died out that time, but more would come. Having to fight against trolls doesn't exactly make life easier when you've been hit by a catastrophe.

Late in the evening in Sweden, still afternoon in the US, we're met by a wave of love—love for Kim and love for us. Kim's friends from all over the world have contributed material to a home page in her memory: www.rememberingkimwall.com.

It's a beautiful, professional-quality website where Kim appears as the gifted, engaged, and well-traveled journalist she was. Here are a number of her articles, here are excerpts from her CV, but above all, here her fantastic friends and colleagues talk about Kim in words and pictures. We read, cry, dry our tears, laugh, cry again. We read about friendship cemented over a beer and sunflower seeds on a balcony on the thirteenth floor of an apartment building in Beijing. We laugh about a rainy Fourth of July in New York where Kim is fascinated by a lonely man under a sun umbrella on a deserted beach.

We smile at the story of Kim leaving a piece of cake in the refrigerator of her vegan host family, convinced nobody will touch it. When it dawns on her a few days later that her family must have thought the cake was a gift and eaten it, she finds herself in a moral dilemma: The cake was made with butter, cream, and eggs. The family thought the cake was so delicious and had asked for the recipe. Should she tell them? We'll never find out what she decided to do.

During the next few days, the web page is filled with more stories and more pictures. Most of them are from close friends, but there are also some from people who never met Kim but who are moved by her fate and want to be in touch. We return again and again to these memories, not least of all during the frightening wee hours of the morning when sleep refuses to come. Here—in the middle of the night—Kim comes back to life again.

CHAPTER 9

In August 1994, it was finally time—Kim was about to start school. After four years at day care, she feels she's done with that life; it's time for a new chapter. The new school bag was packed several weeks ahead of the big day, and her dress has been chosen with great care. She's wearing a blue-striped dress, and her bag is covered with dinosaurs. Miss Catherina has invited the first graders to come sit at their desks and try out their chairs. The pupils' first assignment is to draw a picture of themselves and write their names. Kim enjoys school, but not after-school care. There are too many children there, it's too noisy, and she'd rather sit with a book or draw quietly or continue with whatever she was working on. She's already walking home from school alone in the second grade. She makes herself a snack, does her homework, and then has time for her own activities. She never has any problems motivating herself—she always has some project going. When she doesn't, there are always books. She never goes anywhere without one, and she's always discovering new authors.

As an adult, she loves to read Swedish classics as well as Asian authors. Course books alternate with literature, and a dog-eared paperback is her favorite traveling companion.

During one period Kim reads a series of Indian writers, and in another it's South American essayists who find their place on her nightstand. Peter Hessler's depiction of China acts as an inspiration for Kim's explorations of that vast empire.

After the fall semester of first grade, we are off on a trip to the other side of the globe—Australia. We spend Christmas on Bali, and then we travel to Cairns in northeast Australia. For almost a month, we follow the east coast southward and alternate stays on the continent with visits to the islands in the Great Barrier Reef. It's an experience for all four of us—rain forest, kangaroos, and a visit to a home for orphaned koala bears.

Kim's teacher has given her an assignment. She has to draw and write a book about her experiences. She takes this task very seriously. Once at home, she produces a well-written little book with a lot of facts and lovely drawings. She also gives a report about the rain forest to her classmates, and she does it so well that she's asked to give the same report to the higher classes, too. She doesn't hesitate one moment, and with the help of pictures, the seven-year-old describes life in the rain forest to her older schoolmates. She has really read up on the subject and knows her stuff. Her teacher keeps the book because she thinks it's unique—seldom, perhaps never, has she had a first grader who could create something like this. On her graduation day, Kim gets her book back—her teacher had taken good care of it for twelve years.

Soon we're once again on the road out in the great wide world—this time to the old Swedish colony Saint Barthélemy in the West Indies. We're working on an assignment to create a book about the island and the man who, more than anything else, represents Swedish heritage there: Marius Stakelborough, the descendant of slaves.

Kim sits with us during most of the interviews, listening intently. Marius tells us about his impoverished childhood with his grandmother, about the difficulties of being black, about his struggle for his family.

There are several hours of interviews, but we find we're never yearning for the beach when we're sitting around the table in Marius's backyard.

The weeks in the West Indies form the experience that makes Kim decide to have a life outside of Sweden. Marius's life, his story, and the effect it had on her become the subject of Kim's application essay for Columbia University. We discuss it a lot at the kitchen table at home. It's probably unavoidable, this longing to see the world outside, when you work as a journalist and consume huge amounts of news every day. For most of the time while Kim was growing up, our family read four, sometimes five, daily newspapers. Added to that are the evening papers and a number of weeklies. The television channels add to the mix with even more news—our children live in a constant flood of infor-mation. Some of it probably sticks; quite a bit is probably considered uninteresting. Apart from the confident young child's pronouncements that she'll be a diver or Santa Claus when she grows up, Kim never really articulates what path she will follow in life. On the other hand, she's very clear about which high school she wants to attend: Malmö International School, which is known for its International Baccalaureate (IB) program.

As parents, we only have a vague notion about what this interna-tional education involves, a program that is basically taught entirely in English. We point out rather lamely that she's going to have a long commute to and from school—several hours each day. She gets used to that quite quickly, although it's more than an hour's bus ride in each direction plus several miles of pedaling from the bus stop to school. Day in, day out, rain or shine—for three years. Kim never avoids things that are difficult. Once she decides on something, her path is clear.

From the very first day, IB feels like home to Kim. Here she finds exciting people and the challenges she didn't find in her first nine years of school. We get to hear stories about her new friends, many of them with roots in other parts of the world. During the years at IB, friend-ships are formed that are so strong that many friends become a second family for Kim. They stay in touch through the years despite the distances, sometimes being continents away. For a long time, the only opportunity to see each other in person is Christmas. Once the families have had their share of their particular IB graduate, the group of friends gets together later on Christmas Day.

Graduation day, June 2006: Kim stands with her schoolmates on the steps, cheering and singing. Twelve years of school are behind them, and now their whole lives lie before them. The only thing between the students and their future is their final IB exam grade, which won't be posted for weeks. A good result will give access to universities and other institutions of higher learning worldwide.

It's a long wait, but the grades are finally posted. Kim receives forty-two points out of a possible forty-five. Kim is overjoyed, but not content. She successfully appeals the result, and her grade is changed to forty-three. Even Kim is satisfied then.

In the fall, Kim works in phone sales, selling television subscriptions, a difficult position in which salary is based on sales. But Kim wouldn't have been Kim if she hadn't done a good job. It's not a place, however, where she enjoys what she's doing. After a few months, she enrolls at Lund University. It's no surprise that her main courses are in peace and conflict studies, with instruction in German thrown in for good measure.

In an article in the local paper a few years later, Kim asserts that there are fundamental differences between traditional war and conflicts and those we see in the world today. The subject fascinates her, and she follows developments in the world with interest, especially outside Europe.

Kim starts to investigate different universities, and is drawn to Great Britain. Her field of interest is clear—there's going to be more study of international relations. Kim is called to take an exam in Oxford—a place as British and soaked in academic knowledge as exists anywhere on earth. She spends several days in the classical city of learning and is fascinated by its history, people, and possibilities. One evening she calls home, completely euphoric: "Mamma—guess where I am right now! In Harry Potter's dining hall!" Kim had consumed the books about the young wizard as soon as each one appeared. The films also captured her interest. Now she's in the dining hall that was shown in the film, and she is instantly ten years younger. It's a fantastic experience for her.

She doesn't end up going to Oxford, nor to St. Andrews in Scotland, even though there's a strongly compelling reason—tuition is free there. But three years among the sheep in the Highlands is probably a little too much, Kim thinks, and she decides to become a student at LSE, the London School of Economics and Political Science, in the center of London.

However, Kim can't begin the LSE program midyear, and so she won't move to London to study until the fall semester of 2008.

Until then, her language abilities in English, German, and Spanish are supplemented with French at the Sorbonne in Paris. She travels there without knowing anyone and with the rather useless phrase *"C'est un cheval dans le jardin"* as her only knowledge of French. But as always, she makes her way forward. When her first apartment doesn't work out, she rents a room so minimal that it's without the most basic facilities. She finds a job as a waitress and is cheated several times by tourists who apparently can't read the check. She studies and makes new friends, matures, and learns to live with little money.

In May 2008, Jocke and I sit in the magnificent auditorium at the Sorbonne, proudly watching Kim receive her diploma. Just like all the other graduates, she's wearing the traditional graduation dress, including the hat. That summer Kim travels to India for the first time, together with one of her schoolmates from Malmö and his boyfriend. It's an encounter that will stay with her.

The trio travels through South India, and Kim experiences a world full of colors, sounds, and events, but poverty and misery as well. The difference between rich and poor becomes very obvious to her, and the experiences from this trip will continue to influence her. It's so typical for Kim to take off on an adventure-filled trip to a land far away. When friends her age travel to Rhodes, Ibiza, or some other charter destination, Kim is already, in her mind, on her way to a place far outside the usual travel routes. She isn't interested in nightlife in Ayia Napa; Kim wants to meet people traveling third-class to Thiruvananthapuram.

Meeting people in their own environment, in their homes, getting to listen to their stories, share their everyday lives—this is Kim's way of traveling and experiencing the world.

In August, Kim packs her bag once again and leaves on another adventure, this time alone. Her first year in London she's going to live in a dormitory. Here again she settles in, makes new friends, and gets involved in student life. To supplement her student loans, she works part-time in a café and bakery near the school. It doesn't just give her extra money—it gives her good friends and free coffee, and the latter is not the least important thing. International relations is a subject that suits Kim to a T. In her opinion, it's the most relevant to her choice of profession. Highly placed representatives of world politics often visit LSE. President Obama's black limousine is not an infrequent sight on campus.

Kim loves burying herself in the analysis of world events. But books and lectures are not enough—she becomes secretary of the Nordic Society, with the responsibility of inviting speakers for different events. Her job also includes arranging study trips to countries such as Israel, Palestine, and Lebanon. These trips to the Middle East in particular engage Kim's sense of fairness. She talks about people on the West Bank who have to walk for miles to get water for cooking while the settlers in their neighborhood fill their swimming pools.

It's an exposure to reality that affects Kim deeply. She experiences a similar impact when she participates in the climate conference in

Copenhagen that Christmas. Kim doesn't hesitate to get involved in demonstrations and show what she believes.

The years in London also mean work as a volunteer and as a mentor. Saying no doesn't exist in Kim's world—she asks if she can learn something new from the experience. She throws herself with enthusiasm into a project that uses art to create better relationships between mothers and their children.

Kim spends her second summer break from the university in London as an intern at the Swedish embassy in Canberra, Australia. Usually they don't take on "summer kids," but Kim succeeds in convincing the embassy management to let her come "down under." Apparently, the internship goes well, because after it ends, Kim is offered a shorter term of employment at the embassy. She has several memorable months on the other side of the planet, and she makes friends and relationships for a lifetime. She travels and rediscovers the country that charmed her when she was seven.

Early one morning we get an email from her. The evening before she had been out jogging alone in peaceful Canberra. Suddenly, she felt like someone was following her, a feeling Kim had never had in the sleepy capital. Finally, she gathered her courage and turned around. Her pursuers? A gang of kangaroos.

Even before her work at the embassy, Kim had considered a career in foreign service. One of our family's best friends works as a diplomat, and Kim senses that this could be something for her. It seems her interest in global affairs, her knowledge about international relations, and her desire to discover new people and places make her well suited to work in the service of the kingdom of Sweden.

CHAPTER 10

Thursday, August 24, 2017

Kim's fate is being followed by people all over the world. The newspapers on the other side of the globe are reporting the story. The BBC, the *New York Times*, AP, the *South China Morning Post*, the *Sydney Morning Herald*, *Frankfurter Allgemeine*—the list goes on. Kim's smiling face appears everywhere. Here at home, experts of all kinds are interviewed on TV and in newspapers, and they speculate on what's happened. Some say they know what happened on board the submarine that night. But there's only one person who knows, and he's not saying anything. On the beach in Trelleborg, people gather and light candles in memory of Kim, to share our grief and, maybe, to try to understand. Near our home, one of our neighbors makes a heart of stones. Someone fills it in with the letters *K-I-M*, and others lay flowers there. For us, the stone heart becomes a kind of memorial site, and we pass it several times a day on our walks with Iso. In all its simplicity, this heart is a strong symbol. Then a winter storm comes and takes the stones out to sea with it.

We promise each other that we'll make a new heart in the spring, farther up the beach, safe from the greedy ocean.

Other stones here at home are imbued with great significance. Ole finds a stone with a hole straight through it on one of his visits. He uses it as a key chain, a constant reminder of Kim's home. We find more stones with holes in them on the beach; we collect and take them with us to New York about six weeks later. The little stones, with their holes carved by nature, will be a symbol that touches Kim's friends.

One of Kim's childhood friends writes a heartrending story on Facebook. She tells about how she's just begun swimming lessons with her baby daughter, the same way she and Kim had thirty years ago. She tells about her mischievous, red-haired best friend with whom she had had so much fun.

The next day, the police in Copenhagen announce that they are expanding the charges to include "indecent handling of a corpse," corresponding to what we in Sweden call desecration of a grave.

Friday, August 25, 2017

Kim's friends in New York gather for a memorial ceremony at Columbia University. We follow it online and have the opportunity to share in the joy and sorrow. The gathering is spontaneous—Kim's friends realize that they need each other. A more formal memorial is planned by the university, and we'll make the trip then.

In Ishøj, south of Copenhagen, another event takes place. Hundreds of people come together to participate in a torchlight parade in Kim's memory. None of these people knew Kim, but they take part in a beautiful ceremony anyway. At the end, they throw roses into the ocean.

The attention never seems to end. One day I go into the local store to buy a quart of milk and some bread. At the entrance, I'm confronted with newspaper headlines, one after the other. All are dominated by the picture of our Kim. In wartime font, one expert declares that he knows what happened. It hurts to see our daughter's fate transformed into a reason to buy a paper. I hurry past, but I notice that others see my reaction. A spontaneous hug from the cashier gives me a bit of comfort.

Tuesday, August 29, 2017

In the mail today, a white padded envelope comes from Copenhagen. It's from Kim's friend Eva, who's had a picture framed for us, a photograph she took just a few weeks before Kim was killed. Eva's family has a summer house in northwest Scania, and Kim spent a weekend there amid the beauty of nature. In the photo, it seems like there's a halo around Kim's chestnut hair. It makes us think of the Björn Afzelius song "Isabelle," which he wrote for his daughter. Kim's middle name, Isabel, comes from that very song. The line "The sun shines in your hair, the ground blooms where you walk" sounds almost prophetic. We place the picture on the fireplace mantel in the living room.

We can see the photo every time we walk by, and it's liberating that it's a different picture of Kim—not the search picture we constantly see on television, in newspapers, and on posters. In the envelope sent by Eva, there are a few other photos she took during those days in Arild: Kim playing with a kitten, hamming it up a bit and flashing a big smile for the camera. Kim is happy and content with her life, maybe happier than she's been for a long time. Before her lies a year in China with Ole, a year that will hopefully create an even better platform for her journalistic work. A few weeks earlier, she had brought with her from

New York a kind of confidence we hadn't seen before—editors were now calling her back; her name was known and respected. Now, on her career ladder, the only way is up.

Thursday, August 31, 2017

Many people in Trelleborg are affected by Kim's fate. Pastor Gustaf Centervall creates a condolence book, which is set out at the parish center. The blue book lies open next to a candle and a picture of Kim. We cry as we write the first lines in the book.

When we're given the book two months later, hundreds of people have written messages to Kim and to us. I read it at night when I can't sleep. Just a page or two at a time—I can't take in more.

From Denmark we hear that our request that human remains detection dogs be used in the search has been granted.

Now there are two HRD dogs on boats in Køge Bay trying to catch the scent of Kim's remains. We've been dog owners for more than forty years, so we know what a dog snout is capable of.

Saturday, September 2, 2017

We haven't isolated ourselves since Kim disappeared, but we've avoided large gatherings. Last weekend's street party, the Palm Tree Festival, wasn't difficult to skip. Now, however, we're off to see the people of Trelleborg. For many years, Jocke has performed photographer duties for Harbor Day in Trelleborg, an annual event. Of course I come along. We need each other, and we support each other more than ever. We get through a few difficult hours, but at the same time it feels comforting to encounter all the love that both friends and strangers show us. We're not alone—people are suffering with us. The power of hugs becomes very clear during these hours at Handelskajen Dock. At this moment, they're searching for Kim's remains in Öresund just miles away. Maybe the boats participating in Harbor Day today were out looking for our daughter earlier this week.

In the evening, it's time for the next challenge. I'm the chairwoman of the Old Trelleborg Society. Every fall, we start our year with a kickoff for the fifty or so staunchest members and their families. Canceling the event was never a possibility.

This time we meet them all with hugs and tears, and then move on to a pleasant evening for the invited guests. The catastrophe in the submarine has already hurt us so much—we can't let it prevent others from living their lives as usual. For us, life will never be the same again, but evil cannot be allowed to win. We have to dare to go out and meet life—no matter how painful it is.

Sunday, September 3, 2017

On this Sunday, we become aware of how the tragedy feeds people who may have too active an imagination. An English-language evening paper, published in Denmark, writes that Kim may have been murdered because she was working on an article that dealt with Madsen and a drug-smuggling cartel whose activities span the globe. The paper refers to an anonymous source who supposedly gave the tip to the editors just one week after Kim's death, and it says there's evidence that she was writing an article about the cocaine trade in North, South, and Central America. It also claims that submarines are often used to transport narcotics. Maimed corpses are a sign of South American drug lords, the paper informs us. We never find out if the author is the same person who's also writing things on Twitter, or if it's another troll. Suddenly, a Twitter account pops up called "County Crim Malmö," with a profile picture of Sofia Helin. She's the actress who plays Saga, the police officer in the Danish-Swedish crime series *The Bridge*. The County Crim Malmö tweets claim the same thing as the evening paper, that Kim's death is related to her investigative work on the narcotics trade.

Nobody is aware of Kim ever having written such an article, or that she even found the topic interesting. Shutting down the Twitter account, which has gotten something of a following, doesn't end up being a simple matter, but our new "big family," Kim's close friends, take care of everything. When phone calls and emails to Twitter's offices don't help, some of them go to see them face-to-face. A half hour later, the account is gone.

It's an old-fashioned print newspaper that makes us believe in the goodness of humanity again. *HD-Sydsvenskan* publishes one of Kim's articles from North Korea, split over two issues: "A Tourist in a Closed Country." It ends up being uncomfortably relevant because, since Kim wrote this article, Kim Jong-Un has chosen to increase tests of his nuclear arsenal. This is precisely how Kim wanted to work: to become a voice for the weak and to tell the stories nobody else wanted to write.

Tuesday, September 5, 2017

The prescribed weeks have passed, and it's time for Peter Madsen to be brought before the judge again. Our experience with the Swedish legal system and the detention hearing on August 12 mean that we're pretty certain that the proceedings will take place behind closed doors again. Just in case, I bike home from work—I want to follow the reportage with Jocke.

Long before the scheduled time, the media starts to broadcast. There are teams of reporters gathered on the square in front of the court building.

Microphones and cameras are set up, ready to record what the defense attorney and the prosecutor are willing to share. Swedish,

Norwegian, Danish, and English are spoken into microphones and cell phones. Everyone knows that there'll be a fight for the seats inside—there are entirely too few chairs for far too many reporters. We hear that a French TV crew has been waiting on Nytorvet, the square in front of the courthouse, since eight this morning even though the proceedings won't begin until the afternoon. Most of the journalists probably assume the same thing we do—that the hearing will take place in a closed courtroom. Anything else would be unusual in Denmark. The bell in the city hall tower rings twice, and the hearing begins. We follow it through real-time reporting in the online newspapers—one newspaper on the computer, another on the tablet.

As we expected, the prosecutor requests that the hearing be held behind closed doors. He also orders a mental health examination for Peter Madsen; the police shall be granted access to the man's computer, and he'll be detained for an additional four weeks. Peter Madsen's lawyer protests—why can't her client have the opportunity to speak now when he wishes to do so? The judge grants him the right to speak, and a nearly four-hour-long narration reaches us and the rest of the world. The submarine man tells what happened, how he reacted, what his sexual preferences are. It's difficult, or rather impossible, to take in what we're hearing. The autopsy report is read under what in Denmark is called "report prohibition"—the contents are entirely too violent to be disclosed in public.

Madsen continues to stick to his story: Kim died as a result of an accident, and because he didn't want to have a dead person in his submarine, he buried her at sea. I react strongly to this idea. Burying someone at sea was something that happened during long boat voyages, in a time when there wasn't any way to refrigerate a body. In Öresund in 2017, those conditions don't exist. There's help available a half hour away, at most. There were at least two cell phones on board.

The decision for continued detention is appealed. Madsen's attorney also appeals the decision that her client undergo a mental health examination. Neither succeeds. Madsen will stay behind bars, his computer will be searched, and he'll undergo a forensic psychiatric exam.

We sit in front of our computer with even more questions now. What happened during those evening hours on board the *Nautilus*? Will we ever find out?

CHAPTER 11

In April 2009, Jocke's mother, Helga, leaves this earthly life. She's a bit over eighty, and she's been sick for many years. Kim flies home from London for the funeral, which takes place on Valborg's Eve, April 30. It's one of the first real spring days, and Kim hasn't been home for several months.

Life in London has made an impression on Kim. She glows as she talks about her friends, about school, about long hours, about the demanding pace of study. She's enjoying herself, developing and growing and becoming more confident and focused on her goals. She speaks with true warmth of her job at the café, her new friends, and her plans for the future.

A while later we find her in the big chestnut tree growing on the south side of our house. She's climbed up into what she considers her tree, where there are still big fat buds cradling their leaves inside. They'll be popping open any day now. Here sits Kim, a few yards up in the air, content. Is it being home, even if just for a little while? Is it her life, which is going so well for her? Or is it that Kim was the one who made sure that this tree exists at all?

To find the roots of this chestnut—figuratively—we need to go more than fifty years back in time. Jocke was born in Germany, in the city of

Travemünde, and he grew up near his maternal grandparents' home at Steenkamp. One day Grandpa Albin came and showed the little boy a pot with a plant inside, maybe four inches tall. That fall Albin had taken a chestnut from the garden at the Hotel Kurhaus in Travemünde and planted it in the pot indoors, nurturing it through the winter. Now the tender baby tree was ready to be planted outside the apartment house where they lived. Jocke and Grandpa Albin worked together to plant the little chestnut. The years passed, Grandpa Albin passed away, and Jocke moved to Sweden.

Every time we visit Travemünde, we drive by Steenkamp and look at the tree, which is now magnificent. Ever since the children were small, they've followed along to look at Grandpa Albin's chestnut tree. At some point at the beginning of the '90s, we thought we'd bring a few chestnuts home. We did as Grandpa Albin had done: We made sure that they sprouted, and planted them in pots while we waited for the spring. The children each planted one tree and took responsibility for it.

The story of how the little chestnut from Kurhaus became a tree, which then created new trees in Sweden, made a huge impression on the children.

Many times we heard Kim say that when she grew up and had her own home, she would plant a chestnut tree to continue the tradition.

Kim won't be planting any chestnut trees. But her tree will continue to live and grow. We'll also be able to visualize how she climbs in her own tree next spring and the spring after. The Chinese have a saying: "The one who plants a tree has not lived in vain."

CHAPTER 12

Friday, September 8, 2017

For a few weeks, Kim's friends have worked together with us on a video that will help introduce the Kim Wall Memorial Fund. The whole thing is being done through crowdfunding. Kim's schoolmate and good friend Adam Perez in Los Angeles has done a fantastic job setting up the fund and putting together a video about six minutes long with pictures from Kim's early years, university days, and the present. Our contribution is pictures from Kim's childhood. We've cried and laughed ourselves through endless hours of videos. We got our first video camera when Kim was only two months old. There's as much material as anyone could want, and some of the footage we haven't looked at since it was recorded. We decide on a few segments that show Kim's personality—her determination and her strong will.

Tom got an electric-powered car for Christmas when he was a few years old. It was a green VW bug that he learned to drive like a champ. Kim and Tom had many hours of fun in the yard with it. Usually Kim was the one who directed their activities, and that's what happened in this video segment, too. Tom is driving the car, and Kim rides behind him in a little wagon they tied on with a rope. Kim is bossing her little brother around: Drive here, drive there, faster!

We pull out pictures from when she had just brought home her beloved parakeet, Bobby, and pictures from birthdays and Christmas holidays. Our material is shown together with more recent videos, mostly from her investigative trip to the Marshall Islands. Her colleagues Jan Hendrik Hinzel and Coleen Jose captured Kim just as she was: in the midst of life, in the midst of her work. Kim is so alive, standing there in the pilothouse of a little vessel out in the Pacific Ocean. She talks about her ambitions as a journalist: that she wants to create a space for herself in the male-dominated world of foreign correspondents.

We have no clue whatsoever what will happen once the video is uploaded to the internet, but we wait nervously. Imagine our excitement when, after just a few hours, money starts to trickle in.

The film and its message spread as fast as lightning. As before, we experience the incredible power of social media. It's taken the place of the village well—this is where everything happens now.

After just a couple of weeks, the video has been seen 644,000 times.

Saturday, September 9, 2017

Once again we're shown proof of Kim's ability to make lasting contacts. In Beijing, a large group of her friends and colleagues get together to light candles in her memory. On the other side of the planet, we sit and are warmed by their love. While ABBA plays, Kim's memory is honored. We see and are touched, cry, and feel gratitude for the warmth we are receiving from so many different places on earth.

Friday, September 15, 2017

Now it's been a week since the fund was launched. There are many reactions, and all of them are positive. For us, the fund becomes a way to keep Kim's memory alive—life triumphing over death. In only seven days, the fund has collected $41,123—a remarkable sum. People from all over the world are contributing, from five-dollar donations to large sums.

Wednesday, September 20, 2017

Today we should have been sitting on a plane on its way to Beijing. While she was home during the summer, Kim was planning our first visit to China. She often scolded us for not visiting the country that was so close to her heart.

Jocke's sixty-fifth birthday was as good a reason to go as any, so we were finally going to visit.

Kim told us about everything we were going to do: visit the terracotta army, bike around in the Forbidden City, eat delicious food, and above all, visit the Great Wall—something that has been the source of many jokes throughout the years because of our last name. Kim described the route we would take to get up on top of it, because Jocke's bad knees meant that we needed to make some special preparations. She talked about a man who lived next to the wall and raised chickens. We were going to visit him.

Kim was full of enthusiasm planning our trip, and it was contagious. We were looking forward to seeing China through her eyes. We already knew she was an incredible guide and trip leader because we had traveled with her in India in 2011.

We throw ourselves into practical details to keep our thoughts busy. We now have the resources to make a new video, and this would be the first one in which Jocke and I would appear. The purpose is to recharge interest in the fund in a few weeks. Writing the manuscript isn't the hard part—my heart is full of feelings. But recording the words is more difficult. These words are about Kim, and my voice breaks time and again:

> It was here, on the shores of the Baltic Sea, that Kim Wall grew up. It was here that she played as a kid, building tree houses, collecting pebbles on the beach, and walking the family dog. But the big world attracted her. The many trips abroad the family made during her growing-up years gave Kim an appetite and curiosity for human beings and environments on other continents. After receiving her International Baccalaureate at nineteen, Kim prepared herself for a life with the whole world as her playing field. Studies at the Sorbonne in Paris, London School of Economics, and dual master's degrees at Columbia University in New York made her ready. She worked for six months as a trainee for the European Union in Delhi, India; she served at the Swedish embassy in Canberra, Australia; and she worked for the South China Morning Post in Hong Kong. Kim was particularly focused and determined. Raised in a family of journalists, she was well aware of the advantages and disadvantages of the profession. But there was never any doubt. There were so many stories that Kim would have liked to tell—so many fates that she would have liked the world to hear about. Her ambition took Kim to different parts of the globe. She experienced war tourism in Sri Lanka, the torture chambers of Idi Amin in Uganda, and the ruthless exploitation of environment and people in the South Pacific. But Kim also told us about her fascination with stories that fell through the cracks of news. She reported on odd ways of life in

New York, about IKEA's entry into China, and about women's march for justice. She found stories wherever she traveled; no effort was spared in telling those stories. Kim had a unique ability to see a human being, and she had a genuine interest to tell his or her story.

She did it with great warmth and empathy. At the same time, she kept her journalistic integrity. Kim had a special ability to write a story that could leave the reader spellbound.

Thirty years old, Kim was on her way to establishing herself at the top tier of journalism. She talked about this a great deal during her final summer. After years of effort, hardship, and sacrifice, she was on the verge of taking a new leap. In front of her waited a year in Beijing together with the love of her life. Kim was happy. The future was bright. There were no clouds shrouding her horizon.

Before Kim disappeared, the family gathered to take the yearly family picture. We've done so for thirty years—always in the same spot here in our garden. All of these pictures are on the wall outside Kim's room. There's room for many more there, but there won't be any more photos. Kim isn't coming back to us, but we want to let her soul and crusading spirit live on. It can do just that through her memorial fund—support it and let others continue the work in Kim's spirit. We owe her that.

A colleague mans the camera, and we walk on the beach together with Iso. We gather around the stone heart, look out over the ocean, remember, feel the grief and loss. Jocke sends up his drone to take pictures from above. The heart is easy to see, even from the sky.

Wednesday, October 4, 2017

The Swedish Publicists' Association has called a meeting in Malmö. The topic is press ethics, using the submarine tragedy as a focal point. The editors in chief from *Kvällsposten* and *Sydsvenskan* are on the panel, as is the editor in chief from the Danish *Ekstra Bladet*. Early on, we decide to drive to Malmö—not to participate in the debate, but to hear its tone. The chair of the club shows great understanding for our decision and begins the evening by introducing us and explaining why we are there. The purpose of the debate is to identify differences between Danish and Swedish press ethics. You might think that two countries with just a small stretch of water between them would have similar practices. We've learned the hard way these past weeks that there's a huge difference. And this comparison does not make the Danes look good. Some of the questions we've received from Danish media are ones that few people—and hopefully no Swedish journalists—would ask crime victims: "Can you have the funeral even though they haven't found all the body parts yet?"

Unfortunately, we've also gotten to read articles that express a kind of humor that I don't think Swedish media would publish. A large article is illustrated with images of Kim and Madsen as LEGO figures. Another image shows the submarine man in a poster with a clear reference to the film *The Hunt for Red October*. The editor would probably defend his choice by saying that humor is a way to handle a grim reality.

Maybe there's a deeper psychological significance, but publishing this dark humor at a loved one's expense simply hurts.

The debate this gray October evening never really gets going. There's certainly room for a little self-reflection—it was simply not right to describe the event as an "at-sea burial." Our presence probably cools the participants' desire for debate. Maybe this is a good thing—maybe there will come a time later on when this very important question about morals and ethics can be discussed. We're asked to talk about the fund.

I try to, but I can't do it. My feelings are too strong, and Jocke has to take over.

Here, among old colleagues as well as journalists we don't know, we get a clear message: We aren't alone. Kim's fate has affected the entire profession.

CHAPTER 13

Finally, in June 2011, it's graduation day. By now, Kim has opened the door a crack to the big country in the East that fascinates her so much: China. During her years in London, she studies both Chinese and Japanese in addition to her course requirements. A scholarship gives her a short trip to Beijing, and that's when it happens—Kim and China fall in love with each other. For Kim, the affair would last her whole life. The first seed had already been sown in late winter 1997 when Kim was about to turn ten. The entire family traveled to Hong Kong to experience the country before the United Kingdom turned over control to China. It was a trip full of contrasts—modern skyscrapers, rushing businessmen, and a surplus of Western products in the stores, on the one hand. At the same time, there were houses splitting at the seams with too many residents and snakes in boxes that were skinned live in the gutter once the customer had decided which one he or she wanted to buy. We got to experience the night markets and the restaurants where we had no idea what we were ordering. Kim was fascinated by everything—by the senior citizens practicing qigong in the park, by the collision between Western and traditional, by the sounds, the bustle, the people, and the surroundings.

But China must wait. First there is a completely different challenge to master, in one of the developing countries that had taken large steps toward a higher standard of living. Kim lands a six-month, unpaid internship at the Delegation of the European Union in New Delhi, India. Although she has been accepted into graduate programs at several different universities—including Columbia—she wants to test her wings and her knowledge in the real world. And what could be more real than a half year in India? This is her third trip to the country with which she will eventually develop a love-hate relationship.

Her dream is to get to Asia, and the work at the delegation in India seems promising. Together with a girl from England named Anna, Kim is going to be responsible for reporting on the political situation in the country and the region, and to provide a picture of how this in turn might affect Europe. She must read many English-language newspapers every morning, write analyses and summaries, and ensure that these are ready when the offices in the headquarters in Brussels open for the day. Kim and Anna live with another English girl in New Delhi. They have never met before, but Anna and Kim quickly become best friends. For both of them, this is the first experience with living and working for a longer period in a developing nation, one that is also a nation of so many contrasts.

The half year in New Delhi ends up being intense and exciting, but as Kim hints in her speech at the Foreign Press Association dinner two years later, it also shatters many of her illusions.

As an unpaid intern she gets to see the seamy side of the life of a development worker. India is too much of everything; at the same time, it's a country you can't help but like. Here are all kinds of people—the richest and the poorest. Here you find colors shining so brightly they almost hurt your eyes. Here the cacophony of car and tuk-tuk horns joins with other traffic sounds, and the exhaust and the jams contrast with lush parks and beautiful homes. India is an odd blend of colonial times and modern social development.

Kim throws herself quickly into her work at the EU Delegation. She soon realizes that it's a place with a strict class structure despite the European values that one would expect there. She and Anna are unsalaried and have to pay for their own insurance, rent, and travel. By contrast, the other employees have generous benefits. They can stay for longer periods at hotels, are protected by different kinds of security, have insurance, and enjoy many advantages. The girls find this deeply unjust, as they must use their savings and help from their parents to pay for their safety in a city where attacks on women are an everyday occurrence. There are also large differences in how the young interns are treated by the rest of the staff. Many show them respect and consider them equals; others hardly see them. Even so, Kim's and Anna's work assignments are important and necessary.

Their analyses are sent every morning to Brussels, often encrypted. India and development in the area are of great significance to the future of the Western world.

Kim travels a lot during her time in India. She is able to see large parts of the gigantic country. Almost every weekend, Kim and Anna go off on new adventures. One weekend, it might be the Ganges, the holy river; or another weekend, it might be Jaipur, the "Pink City." Kim becomes charmed by Kerala, the state farthest to the southwest, where pepper grows. It's not just the spices that fascinate Kim—it's also the form of rule in Kerala. In this state, the Marxist-Leninists have had power for a long time. The level of education is higher than in other states, and the standard of living is better. Is it the political system that's responsible for the relatively high quality of life in the area, or are there other reasons? We debate and discuss it without ever coming to a single definitive answer.

During a long weekend, Kim and Anna travel to Kashmir to go skiing. Apparently, it has the highest ski gondola in the world, a fact unknown to most Europeans. As a souvenir, she buys me a necklace with a turquoise stone framed in silver. Even though we're separated by hundreds of miles, we're in each other's thoughts. She knows I will love that piece of jewelry. For Jocke, she buys a fur-lined cap with generous, warm earmuffs. "I don't know what animal it is, but the person who sold it to me swore that it wasn't dog," says Kim with a huge smile as she presents him with the warm headgear.

The conflict-affected areas in the border regions of northern India interest Kim intensely. She studies the area's history and development. She has her analysis ready—the next large war will be about access to water. India needs enormous amounts of water in order to take care of the needs of its population, its agriculture, and its growing industry. The water comes from the mountain ranges in the north and is controlled by another superpower, China. A few years later, Kim will also travel to Nepal and Tibet.

In December 2011, Jocke and I get on a plane to New Delhi. Kim has already told us enthusiastically about everything we'll see and experience together. And we did have two and a half intense weeks in this remarkable country. We travel to Kerala—first on a domestic flight lasting over four hours. The airplane is modern, and the service is at the highest level. A couple of days later, in Kollam, we switch to a far simpler form of transportation. We travel by train, third-class, for pocket change. The experience is amazing, but uncomfortable. We sit on wooden benches, and many of the travelers have large amounts of baggage with them. We eat our lunch during the trip, in the traditional way, using our right hands. Tea merchants with large samovars pass through regularly to offer a cup of chai for five rupees, a price that we tourists find quite reasonable: It's about seven cents.

We leave the train and board boats to travel through the Kerala backwaters, a bit inland.

Rice was once transported on these boats, but now they serve as apartments and are a magnet for tourists. It makes for a magical morning: We come out on the boat's deck before sunrise, hear the noises in the trees around us, cross lily pads, and dock at a small shack to buy fresh eggs for breakfast. We rent a car to get to Jaipur, a life-threatening enterprise. On the main road between New Delhi and Jaipur, large trucks with cargo travel in both directions. The road is edged with cast-off treads from their tires, and makeshift mechanics' garages appear regularly, where cars are repaired under the open sky.

At the border station at Rajasthan, we see Indian clichés personified—men with flutes and snakes that curl up out of woven baskets. I imagine that this is for the benefit of tourists, but it's not something that interests us. We visit forts and palaces, bazaars and modern shopping centers. We travel by tuk-tuk—there, too, risking our lives. We eat delicious food at restaurants that few Westerners ever find. We have the best guide imaginable—Kim puts her entire soul into sharing with us her love-hate for India. She loves the people and the sights, the colors, the cacophony, and the fantastic landscapes. She hates the class differences and the lack of consideration, and she's upset by the racism she sees every day.

On several occasions during our weeks in India, we're impressed by how easily Kim connects with people. She's genuinely interested and curious, and she asks a lot of questions. She observes details and finds things in common to talk about, even with those most difficult to charm. Kim finds the right hotel—never the first and easiest one. She enchants tuk-tuk drivers, she talks to monks in holy sites, and she doesn't give up until we're sitting in the first row to see a traditional theater performance. She never chooses a restaurant randomly, but consults guidebooks and other travelers. And, of course, the trip turns out splendidly—we have a fantastic travel experience with our daughter. She doesn't even raise an eyebrow when we order beer in dry Kerala and it comes to us in teapots. She's seen this before.

We bring Kim's favorites with us in our luggage—precious Swedish foods such as liver pâté, smoked salmon, Kalles Kaviar, and licorice, but that's not all. We also bring around twenty gray T-shirts in various sizes. The shirts were left over after the municipality of Trelleborg had celebrated its 750th birthday four years earlier. They weren't doing any good in the basement of city hall, and I thought maybe they would get some use in India.

On the morning of Christmas Eve, Kim and Anna travel to a temple where they know that the truly poor gather to beg for the day's food. Interest in the gray T-shirts from Trelleborg is so strong that they are gone in a few minutes. It's possible that Kim has images of these impoverished people on her retina when she travels to Sri Lanka later that day with a couple of work colleagues to celebrate Christmas.

We chat in the evening. Jocke, Tom, and I are sitting around the Christmas table in gray, sleet-filled Trelleborg. Kim is enjoying sun and warmth on the other side of the globe. At two in the morning, the phone wakes us up. This isn't usually a good sign, and it wasn't this time, either. Kim and her Italian roommate have been robbed in their hotel room. Maybe a sedating gas was sprayed in, maybe the thief just snuck in very quietly. Their cameras, money, and valuables are gone. Kim is unharmed but angry. She's sat for hours at the police station in vain. The items are gone—it's the camera, however, that upsets her the most. At the same time, she lets drop a comment that the thief was probably poor and needed the money he could get for the European women's belongings. Despite the incident, Kim likes Sri Lanka enormously—the nature and the people. The drawn-out civil war is about to end, a conflict that Kim would return to many times as a reporter. The last Christmas she ever celebrated, she was in Sri Lanka, where she reported on the role of Tamil women in the armed fight against the Sinhalese.

Earlier, in the fall, she had visited Sri Lanka, and as was her custom, she didn't stay at a luxury hotel on the tourist beach. She found her way to the east coast of the teardrop-shaped island, and one day on the beach she met a stray puppy.

She wouldn't have been Kim if she hadn't started to cuddle the enchanting little thing, which, as puppies do, bit her with its sharp little teeth. Kim reacted immediately and visited a clinic to get treated for rabies, which the puppy might have had. Kim was always very careful with vaccinations, malaria medicine, or whatever was needed in the area to which she was traveling. She continued her rabies treatment when she got back to New Delhi, and then she encountered yet another contrast. In the capital she had health care of the highest quality, a modern hospital, no waiting, and doctors trained in the West.

CHAPTER 14

Friday, October 6, 2017

The alarm clock rings early on this Friday morning. I know it's going to be a long day, but I'm still unaware that it's going to be one of the longest of my entire life.

Jocke has a meeting in Copenhagen, so after breakfast and walking the dog, I gather Iso's food, collar, leash, and a can of liver treats. That afternoon we're going to fly to the US, in part to participate in the memorial service at Columbia University. As he has many times before, Iso is going to stay with our good friends who have a farm a bit north of Trelleborg. Iso loves the country life, and we suspect he's always a welcome guest at the Swenssons' home. Just as I'm herding Iso into my Volvo, I get an email from a one-time colleague at *Trelleborgs Allehanda*.

He asks a little cryptically if I'm at city hall—he needs to talk to me face-to-face. I answer quickly: *home, alone, call and we can talk*. A few minutes later, I have Lasse on the line.

What he has to say makes me speechless and teary-eyed: "We've decided to give this year's Culture Prize to Kim. What do you think?"

Trelleborgs Allehanda's Culture Prize is one of the finest awards you can receive in Trelleborg. The recipient in 2016 was film director Jan Troell. This year it will be our daughter, posthumously. The prize money is generous—25,000 Swedish kronor (over $2,500), which will be added to the fund.

I begin to cry, and a strong warmth courses through me. There are wonderful people who dare to think outside the established framework. I promise to say nothing—this must be kept secret until the award ceremony more than a month away.

It's late morning when Iso has been dropped off and I'm driving home across the plain, beautiful in fall colors. Even so, we're happy to be going to New York. Some of our best friends live there, and it's a wonderful city. We've experienced it through Kim's eyes several times, and now her friends will show us sides of the city that we've probably never seen.

Halfway home, my cell phone rings. It's Jocke, on his way from Copenhagen. He's just received a phone call from Jens Møller Jensen—the police have found something in their search of the ocean floor. It's a plastic bag with clothes, probably Kim's. If you can feel any sort of happiness about someone finding your dead daughter's clothes, I suppose I do.

Finally, a breakthrough—it's been almost two months since she disappeared.

Once at home, we try to think about what the bag of clothes means. Madsen claimed that Kim was dressed when he dumped her in the ocean, except for the pieces of clothing that were "torn" off her when he pulled her up through the submarine tower. I don't have time to think any further, when the phone rings again. It's Jens, who has more news for us. The divers have found yet another plastic bag with something in it—they think it's a head. They've also found two human legs lying on the bottom of Køge Bay. The area has been closed off, and they're waiting for the forensic experts. Jens knows that we're on our way to the US together with Ole. We decide that Jens should call when he has more information. He does—when we're standing in the middle of the crowd at security at Kastrup Airport. This is no place to talk about finding human remains. After a brief conversation, Jens makes us promise to call once we've landed in New York. We protest that it will be the middle of the night in Copenhagen, but the police chief insists—we will get news of the find before the press does.

We have plenty of time during the flight to think about the possibilities. We suspect that the media is already on the trail of the new findings, and that the search for interview subjects, us for example, has already begun. It's so nice to be at thirty-five thousand feet and out of everyone's reach. We also know that the new video we've done in order to increase donations to the fund will go online tonight.

Through the video, we'll appear before a large group to talk about our grief and loss for the first time, and we'll explain the purpose of the fund. There's been a need for a statement from us, and now we'll have it—on YouTube and on Facebook.

It takes several hours to get through immigration at JFK. We're Swedes, and we have our papers in order, so we aren't affected by the new, stricter rules for entering the US that have just gone into effect.

At Arrivals, Sorcha and Niall, two of Kim's close friends, greet us. They've waited patiently for several hours and have chosen to spend their Friday evening giving us as soft a start as possible for our days in New York.

During the ride into Manhattan, Sorcha tells us in her melodious Irish accent that she and her friends will be creating a different kind of monument to Kim. The gang usually meets in Prospect Park, since most of them live in Brooklyn, where Kim also once lived. It's been difficult to arrange to meet each other in the huge park—near the balloon seller, at the kiosk—the suggestions have varied. Soon they're going to solve this problem for good. Kim is going to get her own bench in the park, which will become their natural gathering place.

The thought is so beautiful, so smart—Kim would have loved it. "We hope to have the bench ready in time for Kim's birthday in March," Sorcha says as she watches the tears run down my cheeks.

It's late when we get to our friends' apartment in the middle of Manhattan. They've set the table with delicacies and wine, and their welcome is hearty. At the same time, there's something we have to do before we can settle in: call Copenhagen and wake up Jens Møller Jensen at five in the morning. He must already be awake, because he doesn't sound sleepy at all when Jocke calls.

He confirms what he told us previously—it is very likely that it's Kim's remains that have been located. They were found along the route that the submarine took on that Thursday night. The sites also match the markings and finds of the HRD dogs. This patient search has yielded results.

It feels like the pressure on my chest lifts somewhat on this long day. We go to bed accompanied by the sounds of police sirens and traffic, conscious that when we wake up, the whole world will have found out what we know: Kim's remains make clear that what was done to them was intentional, meant to ensure they would stay at the bottom of the ocean.

We've also found out that the cranium shows no traces of injuries from the 150-pound hatch that was supposed to have hit her on the head.

India, 2009

Kim, 1989

Kim and her mother, Ingrid, ride elephants in Hagenbeck Zoo in Germany, 1989

Somewhere in the Middle East, probably 2009

Kim at the Great Wall of China

Kim, spring 2017

Selfie

Graduation joy at the London School of Economics, July 2011

Graduation joy at the London School of Economics, July 2011

Kim in New Delhi, India, fall 2011

Kim with father Joachim's first press photo, published 1967

Kim with her diploma in journalism from Columbia University, May 2013

Graduation ceremony, School of International and Public Affairs at Columbia University, May 2015

Roosevelt Island, New York, with mother, Ingrid, May 2015

Majuro, Marshall Islands, spring 2015

Majuro, Marshall Islands, spring 2015

On board the Lady E in the Pacific Ocean with a fellow passenger

Kim at Runit Dome, Marshall Islands, spring 2015

Kim at Runit Dome, Marshall Islands, spring 2015

Selfie, Christmas 2016

Barcelona, spring 2017

Arild, Sweden, July 2017

Family photo, August 9, 2017

CHAPTER 15

The half year in India had helped Kim make up her mind. Diplomatic life was probably not her first choice. Solidarity, a sense of justice, being able to make a difference—Kim realized that it would be difficult to work according to her primary motivators in the environment she'd experienced during her time at the EU Delegation. Instead, her desire to tell stories, to write, to let her pen do the work in the fight for a better world took over. That fall she would start at Columbia. But first, she would spend the summer in China. She had friends in China from both Sweden and England. Kim felt at home in Beijing, where she found new friends as well as a way to stretch her budget: She gave private lessons in English to Chinese children whose parents felt that having a Western teacher for their little ones was the ultimate in status.

In late summer 2012, we see Kim off—we've lost count of the number of times we've done this. Now she's embarking on her next big adventure.

Getting into the journalism program at Columbia is already a big deal; setting one's sights on a career that's based on a language other than your native one is an even bigger challenge. But Kim never hesitated. The language was no obstacle—on the contrary. Beginning with her first year in high school, English was her main language. After that, she basically only spoke Swedish with those of us in her closest family circle.

Kim finds her first apartment in New York in the International House, which is a bit far from Columbia's enormous campus in upper Manhattan's Morningside Heights neighborhood. It sounds a bit fancier than it is in reality. For $1,000 per month, Kim and her roommates each have a minuscule room of about seventy to seventy-five square feet, a shared bathroom, and not much else. This doesn't bother Kim, however, who doesn't spend much time in her room anyway. Instead, Columbia's School of Journalism—J-School—becomes her new home. She spends all her waking hours there, and it wouldn't surprise us to hear that she spends some of her sleeping hours there as well.

Columbia's policy is to provide the international students with a daylong orientation before their American classmates arrive. All of them are new, nobody knows anyone else, and they come from all corners of the globe. In other words, the first day of school. One of Kim's friends tells us about how he and Kim had become good friends immediately.

He relates how they met that very first day over a common interest in unique, fun things. They shared a taste in music and had a common idol, the rapper Akon. His words and music would follow them through many nights when deadlines threatened and articles needed to be polished.

In just a few short weeks in New York, Kim's curiosity and hunger for news push her out onto the beat. On August 24, Kim and her classmates, the one hundredth class of journalists at Columbia, have just started a three-week introductory course in radio reporting and photography. The course on breaking news reporting wouldn't start until later in the fall.

On this day in August, a fifty-eight-year-old man shoots a former colleague in the area near the Empire State Building. The crime takes place in the middle of the day, on the street, in the midst of people going to work and tourists eager to see the building. The police intervene and shoot the murderer in the street. Kim hears about the event and goes off to the scene after informing her professor. "I told her to be careful, since she didn't have any formal training in how to handle such a situation," Sandy Padwe says. "She's to go there, collect information, and then we'll see what she can do with it later."

Together with her classmate Chris, Kim goes to Thirty-Fourth Street. Chris says that when they arrived, the police had roped off the area. However, this didn't prevent Kim from ducking under the tape and taking her place with the other reporters.

Kim doesn't make an article of it, but of course she brings pictures with her back to school. "That's how I remember Kim," says Professor Padwe. "She was so determined."

Padwe tells another story about Kim: "A few months later, Hurricane Sandy hit New York. I was at home in my apartment when the phone rang late one evening, and once again it was Kim on the line. She had walked from Morningside Heights to Midtown Manhattan. She wondered if I could help her edit an article she had written about what was happening in the city. She had sold the article to one of the English papers—I think it was the *Independent*. One hour later, almost midnight, I got her story. We spent a half hour on it, and afterward she seemed satisfied. And that's how I want to remember Kim: a young student who somehow from the very beginning understood and respected the art of reporting."

Another of Kim's teachers, Karen Stabiner, says this about Kim: "We teach many skills at Columbia, but we can't teach curiosity and hunger, although that's precisely what distinguishes a gifted writer—one who's never satisfied, one who always has one more question to ask. At the beginning of my semester-long course on feature writing, Kim said that she wanted to write unexpected stories, and that's exactly what she did. She took the topics seriously, even if they often made you laugh. The combination of finding odd stories and treating them with respect got her sources to relax and allowed her to get the most out of the interview."

Karen Stabiner tells about Kim's ability to find material for her articles by walking around in the city. "She knew instinctively that the best stories are found face-to-face, not behind a computer screen. Kim was a brave, special, and engaged storyteller—and that is the best compliment I can give anyone."

In November, Kim applies for a stipend to take a reportage trip. One of her teachers, Amy Ellis Nutt, a 2011 Pulitzer Prize winner, writes a letter of recommendation about her student:

> *Kim is an unusual student, one of the quickest to learn that I have ever had the joy to teach—not least of all given her background as a non-native English speaker. Her ability to accept criticism and suggestions, and to use them, make her way of writing stand out.*

The teacher continues to say that Kim has the sensitivity of a mature reporter, an eye for details, and the determination to keep developing. She talks about Kim's impressive knowledge of international relations, economics, and politics, but also about her great curiosity:

> *This passion, which cannot be taught, is constantly present during her education. Kim has reported about a number of different subjects, for example gang activity in a residential area in East Harlem, problems with health insurance among Hispanics and the closure of a cigar shop as a consequence of increased tobacco prices.*

> *All of Kim's competencies and instincts rose to the surface in her way of reacting to Hurricane Sandy. Immediately she grabbed her pen and camera and got her story. She traveled*

to New Jersey and spent hours reporting on the people in Hoboken and the destruction that the flood waves caused. She interviewed the residents, the small business owners and the volunteers, and she had the opportunity to listen to their stories of distrust and how they handled the aftermath of the storm. Her photos were also a gripping and powerful complement to her reportage, which included this sequence:

"'It was like the Colorado River out here,' says Tad Eaton, 46, part owner of an antique store as he cleans up pieces of wood debris outside his store. He points to the street, where the red fire hydrant had been covered by the flood wave's water a couple nights ago. During the storm, Eaton did not leave the store, located in an old horse stall, and escaped to the upper floor when the water flooded in over the floor. With his flashlight he could see how the furniture he had restored, and his refrigerator, were floating in five feet of salt water, and he got ready to evacuate through a window."

CHAPTER 16

Saturday, October 7, 2017

We wake up to the smell of freshly brewed coffee because our good friend Carol is doing everything she can to spoil us. She has been around since before Kim's birth; we became acquainted on the island of Cozumel in Mexico in the fall of 1986. Ever since, she has faithfully sent gifts for every Christmas and birthday, and she acted as extra security for Kim during her years in the US. At home in Scandinavia, Jens Møller Jensen has once again held a news conference and told about the find. The media storm is immediate, and now new chapters of the story are being written—a story that just about every person, at least in Scandinavia, is familiar with.

It feels good to be four thousand miles and six hours away, in a large city where we are completely anonymous. Even if the case has been reported in the large newspapers, nobody knows that we are Kim's family. For the first time in months, we can walk around outdoors without anyone recognizing us. At lunchtime, we'll pick up Kim's belongings in her apartment in Brooklyn. Several of her friends have volunteered to help.

The girl who's renting the loft in the now very trendy part of the city has packed Kim's things. Here are the framed propaganda posters from North Korea, the neon sign with the word *ATOM* that meant so much to Kim, a tiger mask, one more suitcase with a missing wheel, and—of course—a blue IKEA bag. It feels strange to come back to the apartment that was Kim's home for several years. The last time I was here, there were traces of Kim everywhere. A small photo of our whole family hung on the wall in her room, taken at Disney World more than twenty-five years ago. Kim and Tom are sitting in the blue double stroller, with Mom and Dad behind them, smiling. The picture was taken in Florida, copied at a quick-photo stand, and sent home as a postcard to family and friends. The picture had disappeared from my mind a long time ago—we've taken a lot of pictures like that over the years. For Kim it was important, and it followed her from one temporary home to the next. She never said it out loud, but we were obviously in her thoughts. Often.

Now the apartment shows signs of other residents. Kim's life is packed away in suitcases and boxes. Here in Williamsburg, she made her first real home after living in dormitories and renting rooms. For a few years, the fifth floor at 11 South Street was her home. Now, she will never drag heavy bags of laundry up all these stairs or enjoy the sunset from her rooftop terrace. Sadef's car is filled with Kim's things, and a taxi swallows the rest.

After helping us, Kim's friends are heading in different directions, and we're on our way to have lunch with Oliver, Kim's school friend from her Malmö days. They shared an apartment for a year or so in New York—as well as friends, memories, and stories. Some of these memories come up during our meal, and they make us laugh as well as cry. A friendship that lasted almost fifteen years ended that night in Öresund.

Wednesday, October 11, 2017

When I wake up, I have a lump in my stomach. Today I'm going to speak at the Columbia memorial for Kim. We know that many of Kim's friends and teachers have accepted the invitation from the school's dean and that the hall will be full. Columbia's journalism program is the most prestigious in the world, and it is incredibly difficult to gain entrance. Our Kim got in, and she also graduated with honors, a kind of gold star for the best students. Now we'll find her name engraved in the wall with others whose names begin with *W*. The students in the first hundred classes have been honored in this way.

Today, a bit more than four years after her graduation, we've returned. This time it's not to bask in the joy of our daughter's accomplishments, but to remember them with her old classmates and friends. Many have traveled far to show Kim their respect and love. We've requested a light memorial; we want Kim to be remembered for who she was when she was alive—this is our wish. It's not a funeral. It's a time to remember Kim as the human being, friend, colleague, student, daughter, sister, and partner she was.

Before the ceremony begins, pictures of our big new family will be taken in the school lobby. Some of Kim's friends have stayed up half the night to make peace symbols in fluorescent colors, fastened on sticks. This symbol, with the index and middle fingers held up in a V, is Kim's signature gesture. She makes this sign in pictures and videos—the peace sign is her brand. During later years, she used the peace-sign emoji constantly. Another friend was able to find yellow pins with the same symbol. I'm happy and moved, and my feelings make me drop my pin on the floor. Young eyes and eager hands find the little piece of metal, which is quickly fastened to my dress. Despite the circumstances, it's a joyful photo session. There are fifty to sixty of us in the picture. We're smiling, at least on the outside. Our paper peace symbols are held up in the air, and we feel the warmth of each other's closeness. Family and friends have gathered in Kim's honor—she's the common denominator, the hub in our lives.

The ceremony is lovely and dignified. Someone with a great deal of empathy has placed packages of tissues on our reserved seats in the first row. As soon as the video starts to roll, my tears fall uncontrollably. Adam Perez speaks about the dandelion that spreads its seeds all over the world, where they take root. He compares Kim's influence to the seeds of the dandelion. A few months later, he has a dandelion tattooed on his arm, in Kim's memory.

Several of Kim's friends and classmates read excerpts from texts that she wrote. Every one of them wears a yellow peace symbol on their chest. Then it's my turn to go up to the lectern. Jocke comes with me to give me strength. I've practiced my speech many times, both in Swedish and in English. I know that my feelings usually overwhelm me when I get to the end, but now I have to try to get ahold of myself.

My eyes wander over the room full of people. Here and there I see a familiar face—friends from Sweden who live in the US have come to the event. The first part of my speech goes well, and the second part, too. I even hear a few laughs when I talk about Kim's animosity toward ATMs all over the world. But then the last part comes, where I talk about the need for brave women like Kim. Then I can't talk anymore—I have to breathe deeply to get through the last lines. My very last sentence—"Kim, we miss you"—probably can't be heard at all. My words get stuck and my voice cracks. This is the hardest thing I've ever done.

"The one who makes a journey has something to tell." The German journalist and author Matthias Claudius wrote these

*words at the end of the 1800s. This saying describes maybe
better than anything else our Kim. Her entire life has been a
journey, and it has generated a lot of stories. We who have the
benefit of sharing Kim's past for a shorter or longer time know
what a fantastic ability she had for telling us about small and
big issues alike.*

*No matter if it was about the current situation in foreign
policy or the latest trend in vegan cooking, Kim was always
in the know, and she let us share it with her. Already as a kid,
Kim was inventive, persistent, and very determined. When
she thought that the bedtime stories we read to her were far
too short, then she learned to read on her own. Nothing was
impossible—everything should be tested at least once, she
believed. For Kim, there were no boundaries—the world
was hers to discover. In the year 2011, she expressed her future
plans in the local newspaper this way: "I want to know how
the world works and I hope that I maybe one day can learn
enough to make a difference for the better."*

*Born and raised in a family of journalists, Kim was well
aware of the advantages and disadvantages of the profession,
not least of all in these days. But there was never any doubt:
Kim had made the decision that she would become a journalist. The joy in her voice when she told us that she was accepted
to the J-School at Columbia was boundless; the adventure
was to begin.*

*During the years in the US and all the trips around the world,
we've gotten small glimpses of her life: an email, a Skype call,
a request for a small loan when the ATM gobbled her credit
card. Occasionally we got a picture taken on the fly. It could be*

a backpack for cats, an especially beautiful tree, food stalls at the market, or something else that she knew would amaze the old ones at home. Of course we were worried many times. Kim traveled around by train alone in Southern China, rented a motorbike in Burma, and showed fascinated girls in North Korea what to do with nail polish.

The parental worry was some kind of normal condition, but we knew that Kim was careful and didn't take any risks. Those worries were put on hold this summer. Kim was in Copenhagen, a forty-five-minute train ride away from home. Ahead of her waited a year in China with Ole, the love of her life. Several stories were already in the pipeline, contracts written, and the finances somewhat secured. The last assignment in Copenhagen focused on the two Danish space programs, a story about a modern space race in miniature. Kim would interview a submarine constructor who planned to be the first private person in space. A couple of hours of work, then all that remained were the last preparations for the move to China.

Now we have the answer: Kim did not return. There are many questions still to be answered. But we, and the rest of the world, will not get Kim back. Her journey ended here, and we have been deprived of all the untold stories she would have loved to tell us. Humanity needs more courageous women like Kim, women who want to and dare to tell, give their voices to the weak ones, and make this planet a better place to live.

Kim, we miss you.

A number of Kim's teachers speak, telling anecdotes that show the person Kim was. About her stubbornness, her strong will, and her determination. It hurts, but at the same time, it feels good to hear.

She's made such an impression. Kim wasn't a large person on this earth—five foot five and just over 110 pounds—but she's left deep traces in people's hearts. The last person to speak is Tom. He holds up the Muji pen he found on the windowsill in Copenhagen two months ago. He gives a fiery speech that challenges everyone in the room to continue to fight in Kim's spirit, to arm themselves with pens and to use them as swords in the struggle for freedom of speech:

> *It's the tiny things in life that have the largest impact. It's the details that get you, that haunt you, that make even the unfathomable fathomable. Not the big stuff. Not the headlines, nor the bulletins, nor even the calm but serious voice of a police officer. No. It's the fine print, not the bold letters, that makes the unreal seem real. For me, it was when we gathered Kim's belongings from her and her boyfriend's apartment. Her possessions were neatly packed in a couple of blue bags from IKEA and a couple of suitcases. When I grabbed the bags in order to load them into my father's car, my gaze fell on a thin cylinder of transparent plastic. It had a yellow label with some Japanese characters on it, and a bar code. It was a pen of the brand Muji. And Kim swore by them. She didn't just use them with a passion for her writing; she loved them so much that she would, often with success, try and convert others to the brand's greatness.*
>
> *And she would leave them everywhere. Everywhere. You could probably track her many travels across the globe solely by her lost pens. It was with those pens that she would write her stories, using them to jot down the quotes of the various people*

she met. They say that the pen is mightier than the sword. And they might be right. But for Kim, her pen was her sword. And she used her sword not for violence, but for something far more powerful: for telling stories. Armed with nothing but her wits, a notepad, and her trusted Japanese gel-inked ballpoint pen, she gave a voice to those who had something important to say. It was there, in her small room, holding her belongings in two blue bags from IKEA, that it dawned on me: Kim will never wield a pen by Muji again. She will never explain the greatness, the superiority to anyone ever again. Nor will she lose another one, ever again. She will never write a single word ever again. But others might. And that's exactly how we should remember and honor her: by remembering the words that she wrote, what she stood for, and what she believed in, and striving to follow in her footsteps. So let's arm ourselves with our swords and make her proud!

CHAPTER 17

The year at J-School gave Kim friends for life. The bonds that were forged here were so strong that no geographical distance could weaken or break them. The punishing pace of study, high expectations, and the encounter with a large city like New York welded the friends together. Almost all of them were far from home, and they had different religions, skin colors, and backgrounds, but they were all driven by the will and desire to become journalists, to get to tell stories and to be able to make a difference.

One mandatory course was RW1, Reporting and Writing. Each student had an area of town from which they would report. Kim was given—or maybe chose for herself—East Harlem. She made frequent visits to this part of town, where she had to convince her reluctant interview subjects why she wanted to hear their stories in particular. The task was to find news. Kim did that, in different ways. She visited a jail, she interviewed Latin-American musicians, she went to church services and concerts. A service where animals of all kinds were given a blessing became an important part of Kim's reporting.

Viola, one of Kim's friends, says this about her:

Kim taught me a lot—her attitude was that if you wanted to do something, you should just do it! Sometimes we are our

own biggest obstacles. We don't think we're able to do some-
thing, that we're not good enough or we have to ask permission
before we can turn our dreams into reality. Kim didn't ask
permission—she just did it. She didn't hesitate to ask for help,
either. Our chats are full of her questions.

Another friend, Jon, said that Kim never pretended to know something she didn't. "If she didn't get a satisfactory answer, she looked at you and said, 'What? Is that all?'"

For us, Kim's friends have become a new family—a family made up of people from all corners of the world. We have been invited in and embraced, and we've received more warmth and love than we ever dreamed possible. Now we have daily contact with several of Kim's friends. Some playfully call us "extra Mom" and "extra Dad," but it's tragedy that has brought us closer. We've all learned the hard way how quickly life can change. You have to take advantage of the day at hand—tomorrow may not come. Or the tomorrow that comes might look completely different from what you imagined.

During all the years Jocke and I have spent in the newspaper business, it was clear that there was—maybe still is?—competition even between staff members of the same paper. You compete for the best spot on the first page, highest up on the website, or even getting your article on the preview ad.

But Kim and her journalist friends don't work that way. Here, the economy of sharing has made inroads. Freelancers give each other tips about article suggestions, and they work together, even helping each other with grant applications. Maybe the most important thing is that they support each other 100 percent.

CHAPTER 18

Thursday, October 12–Tuesday, October 17, 2017

Our days in the US pass quickly. We meet many people whose paths
have, in some way or another, crossed Kim's. We get to hear testimony
about the power Kim had as a professional, and about her ability to seek
out the proverbial silver lining whenever she could. We meet the board
of the CPJ and get a glimpse of the important work they are doing.
For journalists active in Sweden, it's sometimes difficult to understand
that the work conditions for colleagues around the world look entirely
different. At home in Sweden, we've done our best to prepare ourselves
for the meeting with the IWMF—the organization that will administer
Kim's fund. Whom will we meet? How will we present our wishes, and
how can we maintain Kim's name in the best possible way? Once again,
we're met by big hugs, a lot of warmth, and love. The women we meet,
over American pancakes and constantly refilled coffee cups, share our
involvement and our will. The fund will become the tool that ensures
that Kim's work is not forgotten.

The previous weekend we had gotten proof that what we're doing is right—the fund had reached $100,000! The happy news is spread quickly all over the world—from New York to Los Angeles, from Beijing to the South Pacific. Now we know that the fund can distribute money for a long time to come. But now, encouraged by our success, we decide we want more. We raise the goal to $200,000—if we meet this goal, the fund can outlive us.

We've been in New York many times, but we've never visited Wall Street. Now we do, drawn there by the statue of the small girl challenging the large bull. Once we're there, we're hit by the feeling that this bold little girl is Kim. She, too, dared to stand up against the world when she felt that she was right and the world was wrong. We spend a lot of time with Kim's friends, eating dinner together at restaurants that Kim enjoyed.

We talk and talk—memories, anecdotes. Kim's with us, even though she's not. Although she's been gone for two months, she feels more alive than she has for a while. It's comforting, but it doesn't succeed in filling the big dark hole in my chest. *Unfair* is the word that keeps coming back. Why didn't she get to continue her life?

Wednesday, October 18, 2017

We're invited to the IWMF's large annual event, the Courage in Journalism Awards, a prize for brave women in journalism. Although we've never been to an event like this before, we've seen them on TV and in films. It's very American—"everybody who's anybody" in the industry is there. And we are, too. We don't know anybody, and we don't think anyone knows us. We're not prepared to see Kim honored through a display of her picture on the large screen onstage. Famous television personalities mention her by name in their speeches. So beautiful—so sad.

During the fall, there are several more public events where Kim plays one of the main roles. At a CPJ event, Meryl Streep mentions her name. Several of Kim's colleagues win prestigious prizes and claim them in Kim's name. We're constantly reminded that journalism is a dangerous profession, and not only in countries torn by war. In Europe, five journalists have lost their lives this year while at work.

Kim is nominated, among around thirty other journalists, for the Prix Europa, which is awarded in Berlin. The prize goes to a Turkish reporter, but Kim's name, too, is mentioned all over the continent. When the Stora Journalistpriset (Sweden's Grand Prize for Journalism) is awarded in Stockholm at the end of November, Kim is one of the journalists honored. We wish so deeply that the recognition didn't have to come at this price.

When we come home from the US, there's a package slip in the mail, a registered letter. We're not expecting anything—a registered letter usually means something like a driver's license. When we go to pick it up, we're given a large package from England. We don't know the sender, but our address is correctly and neatly written on the box. We open it at home and find the loveliest condolence book you can imagine. Some of Kim's friends from London have spent many hours creating a scrapbook in which Kim speaks to us from each page. Letters, pictures, stories—this is a book so full of love that you can almost feel it physically. Some people—people unknown to us—have created this book to soothe our pain and sorrow. Once more we're overwhelmed by the humanity that we encounter. The book is wonderful, just like its contents. I'm only able to read a little at a time.

Martin writes: *I wish we had had more time together. In my thoughts you were going to be my friend for my entire life. But I'm carrying you with me in all the small jokes and all the strange expressions you planted in me.*

What Leonor remembers about Kim is her laugh, so infectious that you couldn't help laughing yourself.

Eva writes about Kim's brick-heavy Mulberry bag, as well as the questions she would have asked her—the subject of the book she was going to write, the curry dish in Sri Lanka, and the pride Kim had in what she had achieved.

During the long hours of the night, our cat, Leo, often keeps me company in the living room. He rubs his silver-gray fur against my bare legs; maybe he's trying to comfort me. The only reason he's here in our house is thanks to Kim—although we didn't see things that way in the summer of 2005.

Kim had been at the SommarRock Svedala Festival with a friend, and she was going to sleep over at his apartment in Malmö. On this late Saturday night, she finds a gray cat on Amiralsgatan. Probably without considering the consequences at all, Kim rescues the cat. That's how she was—the protectress of all things living. The next morning she calls us and tells us about the beautiful abandoned cat. "Over our dead bodies," we say before she can even ask. "We have a dog and we don't want a cat. Put up notices in the area, call the police, but don't bring the cat here!" Two days later, we hear a noise from Kim's room. She isn't home, so we open the door. In the middle of her bed, the little cat is meowing pitifully. Kim has given it food and water and tried to hide it from us. "I couldn't just leave him on the street!" Kim says in her own defense. "He would have been run over by a car!"

Of course we fall for the cat's pleading eyes, and now he's been a natural part of our family for a long time. Later on, we hear that Kim had had the cat under her arm during the bus ride from Malmö, and the whole time he made no attempt to escape. He knew that this human was someone with a big heart for animals like him. Leo has always been a shy cat, but every time Kim came home—even after many months away—he appeared and rubbed himself against her legs. He knew who his mistress was.

During the fall, he goes into Kim's room often and curls up on her bed. I don't know if it's because he wants to be left alone, or because he misses Kim.

Thursday, October 26, 2017

After two months in the congregation building in Trelleborg, the blue condolence book finds its way to us, and we get to read all the beautiful words and thoughts that the people of Trelleborg, and others, have written there. On the outside, it's a simple blue book, but what's between its covers is unbelievable. Young and old, people who know Kim and us, as well as people who are complete strangers—all of them have tried, in their various ways, to capture their grief and ours in words.

The truth is that Kim had "disappeared" from Trelleborg years ago, when she started high school in Malmö at sixteen. Three years later, she moved first to Lund, then to Malmö, Paris, London, and New York. Her contacts with old friends from Trelleborg became weaker and weaker, for understandable reasons. Even so, hundreds of people have expressed their feelings for Kim, for us, and about the tragedy that everyone has become a participant in. *Kim was one of us—we share the sorrow,* is what I seem to read in the pages of this book. The blue book becomes my companion during the scariest hours in the middle of the night. I read a few pages, cry, think, remember, and put it down. It hurts so much—but at the same time, it's the finest gift you can receive. It's on the table in the living room next to Kim's picture and a small angel we received as a gift. A few short excerpts:

All our warmth and love to you.

The world is horrible.

There are no words.

Thank you for everything you did for many people despite your short life.

We want to give you words of comfort but we can't find any.

Why?

That an important flame should turn to ash. So wrong, so unnecessary, so incomprehensible.

During the fall, we get more examples of Kim's ability to make an impression on people. Her friend and schoolmate Anna runs the New York City Marathon—for Kim's sake. In 2016, Anna had run in the same competition, and that time Kim was standing at the finish line, ready to congratulate her and take her out for a drink.

Joel, the head of the CPJ, writes an email that goes straight to the heart. During our visit a few weeks earlier, we had given them an enlargement of Kim's portrait. Joel has had the picture framed, and now it goes from desk to desk in the organization's office in Manhattan. The one who's made the most meaningful contribution to the safety of journalists gets to have Kim's picture on their desk—to give strength and inspiration.

CHAPTER 19

There are many tales from Kim's years at Columbia. One was how she got out to Long Island and reported on the people who lost their homes and all their possessions during Hurricane Sandy. Others featured long nights at the school, parties, and karaoke evenings. Kim enjoyed herself, soaked up knowledge like a sponge, and became more and more convinced that she had found her place in the world. Here Kim found her journalistic work method, which she herself chose to call "shoe-leather reporting"—wearing it out on the streets while looking for stories. Meeting people where they live—getting the nuances, body language, and environment. She never gave up this way of working. Of course it would have been easier to pick up the phone or surf the internet, but that's not how Kim did things.

We flew over to New York for graduation, of course, which took place on the large campus in May 2013. We hadn't seen Kim since the summer before; we'd only talked on the phone and kept in close contact by email. Naturally, we couldn't wait to hug her. We finally got to, but not until late in the evening—the students were meeting until the last minute. Kim was glowing with happiness when we met her on the rooftop terrace on the seventeenth floor of the building where our good friend Carol lives. She was bubbling with joy, talking about this and that, and looking forward to the next day when she would stand in her blue academic gown with the insignia that showed that she had earned her master's degree.

It was a magnificent event outdoors at Columbia the next day. Class after class was shown to their place, and each had some item that represented their department. Kim's class waved newspapers, of course. When the whole thing was over, and Frank Sinatra's great hit "New York, New York" was booming out of the speakers, we gathered to eat lunch. Everywhere there were students, all on their way out into their adult working lives, most of them filled with uncertainty. In the afternoon, the journalism students had their own graduation ceremony. What Kim was most nervous about was that she would trip in her rather high heels, but of course everything went just fine, and she received her diploma from Professor Padwe's hand. Even Kim was satisfied when she posed with her diploma, her father behind the camera.

The next day, another chapter was about to begin in Kim's life as a journalist. She had landed an internship with the *South China Morning Post* in Hong Kong. She was looking forward to going to China again, even though it was in another part of the huge country. Hong Kong would end up being something of a disappointment for Kim. She felt rather lonely in the gigantic metropolis, which she thought was entirely too Western. She missed genuine Chinese-ness, and she was homesick at least once, a feeling that otherwise was foreign to Kim. Midsummer Eve came, and in order to cure her acute need for Swedish summer, she went to IKEA and purchased a jar of herring and a small bottle of aquavit.

In that way, she had something of a holiday, anyway. The work at the *South China Morning Post* was interesting, but I think Kim missed the feeling of being out on the street meeting people. It was that part of the job that she liked the best. Now she mostly sat summarizing and analyzing in front of a computer screen.

In May, the whistleblower Edward Snowden fled to Hong Kong. He had been employed by the Central Intelligence Agency and worked as a consultant for the National Security Agency in the US. Snowden leaked confidential documents that showed that the US and Great Britain were conducting hacking attacks against operations all over the world. Snowden turned over his material to the *Guardian* and the *Washington Post* before he escaped from Hong Kong.

Her newspaper wrote about Snowden, of course, but the assignment didn't go to the paper's youngest intern. Soon after, Kim was offered continued employment with the *South China Morning Post*, but now she wanted to move on. She had gotten wind of a story in Sri Lanka, and that's where she went next. Now she and Anna were going to tackle the destination that the guidebook giant *Lonely Planet* said was the best of 2013. Kim was critical—making the bloody civil war a tourist attraction was something she considered immoral, and she wanted to let the world know.

She thought it would be easy to sell an article about such a controversial topic. In an email to us, Kim writes: *This is totally important, but nobody cares since Sri Lanka doesn't have any oil*. This is how she briefly described her own proposed report in a pitch to a newspaper:

> *Is Sri Lanka's regime using tourism to whitewash its war crimes? While Sri Lanka's beaches, animal life, and Buddhist temples have made the island a popular tourist destination for foreign visitors, a very different tourist industry has blossomed in secret.*

Kim goes on to say that bus tours are arranged for Sinhalese to the Tamil area in the north. The victor in the long-drawn-out civil war wants to look at what's called the Killing Fields. Bunkers and fortifications have become tourist attractions. Four years after the end of the war, Sinhalese tourists can freely visit and exploit an area in the north that was previously impossible to access. They come in full buses on newly built highways that are bordered by what Kim calls macabre war monuments that celebrate what the government in 2009 calls the "humanitarian operation" that "liberated Sri Lanka from terrorism."

Kim had previously described to me the white beaches, which are full of shoes and bleached pieces of clothing. Here, a bit removed from the tourist paths, tens of thousands of civilians were murdered in what was called the safety zone. On the beach, both civilians and militant fighters—Tamil Tigers—were killed; no distinction was made. There are no memorial stones here. When a priest tried to place a cross in his garden to honor twenty-five victims and colleagues, it was taken away and disappeared. Kim was particularly moved by the small children's shoes she found on the beach.

Kim visited a wharf for submarine construction, a jail for Tamil Tigers, a museum for homemade weapons, as well as hotels, and cafés run by soldiers. She talked to high military officials and people in the tourist industry. The account of how the victor does not only write the story but also exploits it for his own profit had a huge effect on Kim. She would later return to Sri Lanka to drill deeper into the fate of the Tamil Tigers. She spent her entire last December in 2016 on the island interviewing female soldiers. Their story was Kim's last report and was published in the spring of 2018. She writes about riveting human experiences—the woman whose leg was blown off by a mine leaves nobody unmoved.

Kim's involvement was also noticed by others, and maybe it played a role in the healing process of the country, long harrowed by civil war. Fred Carver worked for the Sri Lanka Campaign between 2011 and 2016. Today, he's the head of policy for the United Nations in the United Kingdom.

He talks about how he had to deal with many cases in which journalists were exposed to violence, threats, and other harassment. One result of the persecution was that printing presses were burned and journalists disappeared, sometimes for long periods.

"Despite this grim state of affairs, I was exceptionally fortunate in being able to say that none of the journalists I knew personally through my work in Sri Lanka had been disappeared or killed—until now," writes Fred Carver in a tribute to Kim on the Sri Lanka Campaign's website in the beginning of September 2017, a few weeks after Kim's death.

Fred says that he met Kim on various occasions and had frequent email correspondence with her. He describes how he admired Kim, and he hopes that she will be remembered as one of the most brave and principled international journalists that observed Sri Lanka during the country's postwar period. He goes on to say: "Her pioneering work shining a light on the situation in the country's heavily militarized North owed much to her bravery, but also to her great warmth and affability."

Fred Carver also reveals one of the secrets to Kim's success. Her method was often to dress as a tourist and claim she had gotten lost if she was stopped after getting through the authorities' roadblocks. Fred thinks that her disarming friendliness, her age, and her gender meant that many underestimated Kim, which gave her access to places and people that were otherwise difficult to reach. Kim wrote about tourism in northern Sri Lanka during a time when it was strictly forbidden for outsiders to leave the beaten path in general and to visit the war memorials in the north in particular.

Fred Carver writes:

> In so doing she helped prove how pointless the Government's attempts to keep foreigners away from the North were, and it was perhaps no coincidence that restrictions were relaxed shortly afterwards. This paved the way for a number of others to follow in her footsteps, but despite having easier access, few matched her insight . . . Kim was always incredibly helpful, and generous with her time, even when she gained no

advantage from doing so. In my experience, and in contrast
to a fair number of journalists, the support she received from
activists and NGO workers was never taken for granted. The
Sri Lanka Campaign, and I'm sure many others, benefitted
hugely from her support: facilitating contact with colleagues
at other publications, sharing information, and giving advice
on placing stories in the media. She was also incredibly [col-
legial], seeing other journalists as allies rather than rivals, and
happily supporting those working on similar stories.

When Kim left Sri Lanka, she didn't come home. Instead, she went to India once again, to the northern parts of the country. During this trip, she decides to study for another year and get a second master's degree—this time in international studies. She makes this decision when she is far away from civilization, so once again it falls to us to make sure that the application fee is paid. And once again Kim decides to continue her studies at Columbia, although this time at SIPA—the School of International and Public Affairs.

We dust off the old fax machine, get it to work, and are able to pay the first part of the sizable tuition on time. As with other Ivy League schools, studying at SIPA costs a fortune. But Kim is lucky and receives a large scholarship this time as well. Maybe it's now that Kim develops her ability to write successful applications. Through her years of academic studies, she was able to land several stipends for studying, as well as for reporting trips. Without this support, it wouldn't have been possible for her to study further and go on her trips to faraway destinations. Although her national study subsidy was used to the last crown, it wasn't enough for an ambitious student like Kim.

During her trip to India, Kim is able to write a story about a subject that is close to her heart—the poaching of tigers. Tigers have always been one of Kim's favorite animals, and now she's found a new angle. Poor people who previously poached in order to make a living have instead been given a chance to work on a wildlife preserve, taking care of tigers and preventing poaching. But they pay a high price, because they are often rejected by their families. Kim's reportage for the online publication Roads & Kingdoms described in heart-wrenching detail the story of a boy called Rajesh (a pseudonym) killing his first tiger with his fellow villagers. Some twenty years later, markets still exist for almost all aspects of a tiger's body, predominantly in China, though the routes the animals' remains take to get there are circuitous.

That year, she spends the late fall in New York; one reason is so that she can find an apartment for herself and Oddur, her close friend since her time in London.

Now it's time to find a stable base, Kim writes. *I'm so tired of living in other people's houses, sleeping on a couch, and having all of my belongings in a suitcase. We've even bought lunchboxes so we can take our lunch to school.*

The young people finally find a fantastic apartment in the Williamsburg section of Brooklyn. Fifth floor, no elevator, and the rent is astronomical—but Kim and Oddur are convinced that the area will be just the right place to live. And, of course, they end up being right.

Four years later, 11 South Street is an attractive address. By then, the building has also been equipped with an elevator, so the residents no longer have to drag their laundry baskets and grocery bags up the many stairs. Kim spends Christmas at home, after a stop along the way to see the northern lights in Iceland. When she arrives home at Gislöv Beach, she brings stories about Iceland's twelve Christmas elves—strange to us. And they're not nice elves, either. Kim was also given a pair of red socks as a gift, and if we understand correctly, you wear them so you don't annoy the Christmas cat.

Kim brings not only a lot of memories and stories home to us and her little brother, but she's also dragged a big crate all the way from Brooklyn, through all the airport security checks and plane changes. It's a home brewery kit as well as beer from the Brooklyn Brewery for Tom. It's such a typical Kim gift: She knows how happy Tom will be to get it, and that makes all the inconvenience of bringing it over worthwhile. For us she has a similarly thoughtful present, a huge book about apartheid, among other things. It, too, is heavy, but she knew it would be a fantastic gift for me since I've been engaged with the South African issue for thirty years, ever since I went there for the first time. She has dragged all this along with all her suitcases. Sometimes they weigh more than Kim herself, but she doesn't complain.

CHAPTER 20

Monday, October 30, 2017

"Now it can't get any worse." We've told ourselves that many times. Each time we've been proven wrong. Today we learn that Peter Madsen has recently admitted that he butchered Kim's body. However, he continues to deny that he killed her. The charges are expanded to include "sexual crimes under particularly aggravating circumstances." We don't really know what that means, and we don't want to think that thought to its conclusion. The knife wounds to the groin speak for themselves. During the day, we can focus on practical things to push away the gruesome pictures, but at night there's no mercy. The brain ruthlessly creates images of what might have happened down there in the metal hull. If we're lucky, we have a couple of hours of uneasy sleep.

During our trip to the US, the #MeToo avalanche dragged along representatives from virtually every professional group. As for myself, I don't hesitate to sign #deadline, the Swedish media's #MeToo. A long professional life as a female journalist has, unfortunately, provided me with such experiences as well. The connection between #MeToo and Kim is also obvious to many.

Even in the first days after Kim's disappearance, we and her friends heard the insinuations—why wear a skirt on a submarine? Journalists are a vulnerable group, and freelance journalists even more so. Add to that being a young female freelancer. Is a woman supposed to refrain from doing her job? Haven't we come any further in our struggle for equality, even here in Scandinavia? Many female journalists, both those who knew Kim and those who never met her, have spoken up: "We would have gone out in the submarine, too—we would have done exactly the same thing. That could have been me!"

Kim's relationship with Madsen was strictly professional. They had never met before—the agreement about the interview was done by email, and the entire conversation has been saved. Kim was in no way naïve. She took karate lessons as a child, and she had had training in how to handle violent situations. She had radar for dangerous situations.

CHAPTER 21

Kim's studies at SIPA aren't as challenging as those at the J-School. She's also not as fascinated by the subject—what she wants to do is write! Even so, she realizes that with a double master's she'll be more attractive in the job market. People will know that she doesn't just have writing skills, but also the theoretical background for understanding why the world looks the way it does.

The apartment in Williamsburg becomes the focus of her life. Here she gets together with friends, studies, and lives a more circumscribed life than before. She and Oddur go hunting for furniture and other furnishings. They buy some of them at secondhand stores and others they find in dumpsters or on the street. Slowly but surely, they build a life in the pleasant apartment. They each have their own bedroom, and they rent out the third to help with the bills.

During the spring, one of Kim's dream trips becomes a reality—she goes to North Korea. She was supposed to go the year before, but the trip was postponed for security reasons. Developments in the closed country were considered too troubling for Kim to make the trip. She was disappointed, but she understood. Now, however, she is finally going to go. Oddur, Kim, and about ten others leave for the country that is so different in so many ways from what they are accustomed to. Kim is enthusiastic, but I'm worried after reading and seeing how people are treated on the northern half of the Korean peninsula. Test detonations of atomic bombs and missiles don't help my nerves any. There's only one airline that flies to P'yŏngyang, once per day, and the plane goes from Beijing to North Korea. For ten days Kim and her traveling companions see the image that North Korea wants to display to Westerners.

In an article published in the *Atlantic*, Kim tells about her encounter with the closed country that is now trying to attract Western tourists. She talks about extravagant projects such as a ski resort with nine slopes, lifts, and its builders' dreams of international competitions. She writes about a water park, a dolphinarium, and plans for an underwater hotel. Kim describes how even in the bus on the way from the airport, they get to hear that they have nothing to fear in this country, but that there are two basic rules to follow: no disrespecting the leaders and no photographing the military. The first stop is to see the statues of the country's founder, Kim Il-Sung, and his son Kim Jong Il.

As other tourist groups do, Kim and her travel companions stay at the Yanggakdo International Hotel in P'yŏngyang. There are glass elevators, a revolving restaurant, a casino, and a beauty salon. A Western tourist lacks for nothing. Kim also writes about how the capital is decked out as if it's a museum dedicated to the Cold War.

Kim describes a meeting with a young waitress in a water park. In poor English, the seventeen-year-old asks Kim about her age, family, homeland—until her vocabulary runs out and she simply smiles. At a remote rest stop in the mountains, a group of shy women come forward to play with Kim's hair as they explain to the interpreter that she is the first foreigner they have ever seen in real life. Previously, they had only seen Westerners in films. The visit gives Kim a deeper understanding of people who live under entirely different conditions than she does. But Kim had the ability to see both black and white, light and darkness. Of course she sees through the propaganda's dogma, but she also sees the people, their lives, dreams, and hopes. Once at home, she tells us about a strange meeting with a few young girls, maybe a little younger than she was. They had never seen nail polish before, and they were deeply fascinated by it.

She showed them her red nails, and I'm sure she enjoyed the moment when she got to give the girls a glimpse of Western vanity. When they returned to the US, Kim and Oddur took back with them a number of propaganda posters in the classic style. The posters were framed and ended up on the walls in the apartment in Williamsburg, where Kim happily bragged that they had the largest collection of North Korean proletarian art outside of the closed country. Kim and Oddur had also bought themselves uniforms on their trip. They posted pictures of themselves wearing them on Facebook and Instagram with the caption *Back from the DPRK: safe, sound & reeducated.*

The visit, however, had given Kim an appetite for more. She had plans to return to run in the P'yŏngyang Marathon. It would have been an adventure entirely in her style, and what a story it would have been. After North Korea, several other adventures awaited her in Asia: a boat to Japan, a train through the islands, a motorcycle trip through Myanmar—and, of course, India for a few weeks.

Kim writes to one of her friends in New York: *Back soon, bringing North Korean ginseng vodka and Burmese palm sugar cigars.*

CHAPTER 22

Thursday, November 16, 2017

It's just as dark and gray as it can be on a Thursday evening in November in Trelleborg, Sweden's southernmost city. It feels as if all of Trelleborg is present in Söderslätt Hall tonight. It's the eleventh time the Trelleborg Gala has taken place, an event that honors the year's most prominent figures in business, culture, sports, social issues, club activities, and rural development. For the first time, I'm attending the gala as a civilian—every other year, I've worked as a member of the team that arranges it. Now I'm sitting at *Trelleborgs Allehanda*'s table with Jocke, Tom, and Ole. After a while it's time for our editor in chief, Martin Falkenby, and reporter Lasse Thulin to step up onstage to announce who will receive *Trelleborgs Allehanda*'s Culture Prize. The hall falls silent as Lasse begins to speak:

> *Oh, how I wish this could have been different. The circum-stances are extraordinary. We award the prize this year with very heavy hearts. That's because the winner isn't here.*

But it's to celebrate her ideals of the joy of discovery and her
zeal for improving the world, and it's because her spirit of
exciting, fun, big-eyed reporting will live on, that we award
the prize this year to Kim Wall, and furthermore to the fund
that works in her spirit for precisely these purposes.

At this moment, five hundred citizens of Trelleborg, all dressed to
the nines, rise up as one and begin to applaud. For a very long time.
The applause never seems to end. This spontaneous celebration of Kim
makes us weep, as it does many of the guests, along with the prize givers.
The warmth and love that fill this large sports hall is, in this moment,
so very tangible. Adam's video starts to roll, and once again we get to
see Kim as she directs her little brother in the green car at home in our
yard. We get to hear her tell about her work method—being out in
the field, wearing out her shoes, meeting people in the middle of their
reality. Gradually, Lasse begins to speak again. He, too, is overwhelmed
by the expression of sympathy that the announcement has generated:

Many of you know the Wall family and have suffered with
them this fall. I remember the first time I heard that Kim had
gotten an article published in the New York Times. "NYT"
. . . [D]o you hear how that sounds? It wasn't that Kim was
not interested in her home turf—that would have certainly
come with the years. It's just that the big, wide world was so
much more exciting.

And she wrote so well, and reported with such sensitivity . . .
Here I sat at my desk in Trelleborg while Kim was in Uganda,
North Korea, or the Bikini Islands and was living the adven-
tures of Tintin. I was so envious. The thing is that we CAN
do something. Kim was unique, but we can send one hundred
girls out into the world who are like her and who will do the

same thing—understand the world and make it better. This is what we wrote in the explanation of our choice for the award: for a brave and keen voice, curious about the world, that should never be silenced.

CHAPTER 23

I reach Kim just as she is boarding a plane to Yangon in Myanmar, en route to Mumbai. I have sad news for her—her beloved grandmother Lilly has passed away. It was hardly a surprise for us or for Kim—my mother was almost ninety years old. Nevertheless, she was clearheaded up to the end. The day before, Friday, she had talked about how she wanted her funeral to be. It was very important to Lilly that it wait until Kim was back home in Sweden. Kim had to be there—that was more important than hymns and the death announcement.

Kim and Lilly—or rather, Mumlan and Mormor—had a special bond. For Mormor, Kim was never anything but her deeply beloved Mumlan. Early on, everyone else in our family was strictly told that her name was Kim, nothing else. There was, however, once exception: Mormor. It made our hearts warm to hear the elderly lady talk about her adult grandchild, who had traveled the world, using her nickname.

Lilly had always had an artistic bent, and she developed it primarily through ceramics. Many, many times, Kim got to sit at her side at the potter's wheel with her own lump of clay. It soon became apparent that she had inherited her grandmother's talent. Kim made a self-portrait in clay at some point during middle school—a full-length figure of a young girl. Another piece, made at the same time, won Kim the honor of representing Sweden at an art exhibit at the Rundetaarn in

Copenhagen. Kim created a figure in clay of Jesus mounted on a back-ground of human faces. The jury fell for her creation, and, together with the work of other teenagers from both sides of Öresund, her con-tribution was publicly displayed. Kim thought it was embarrassing to have the local paper write about her—typical for a fourteen-year-old. In 2017, during Kim's final summer, her interest in ceramics returned—probably because she and Ole had found a ceramics studio near their apartment. For Kim, memories of those times she spent with Mormor came to life again. We looked for Lilly's pieces at home, and Kim took a lantern back to Denmark with her. The lantern was both a remem-brance of her beloved grandmother and a reminder of a passion for creation that united them both.

Mormor and Mumlan had a relationship that was all their own. Lilly was born in 1925 and Kim in 1987, but the sixty-two years between them created no barrier. On the contrary. I often heard that Mormor was more modern in her way of thinking than I was: Mormor under-stood music better, Mormor was more liberal on different issues. They could talk for hours about everything between heaven and earth.

Kim was very careful to keep Mormor updated about what was happening in her life. After one of her first longer trips to China, Kim made an album of her best photographs. They could sit for hours going over its pages. Kim talked about the photos, and Mormor listened. They met in the stories, and Mormor was able to feel she was there. During the long periods when Kim was abroad, Mormor could see where her granddaughter was in an old atlas. She read the newspapers and kept up-to-date with what was happening in the part of the world where Kim happened to be. Kim's odysseys enriched Lilly's final years, and she enjoyed telling her friends at the rest home, with deep pride in her voice, about her clever granddaughter.

As soon as Kim got home to Sweden after a trip, a visit with Mormor was a high priority. She knew how her grandmother waited eagerly to see her. Mormor was, of course, worried many times when

Kim was out traveling, but she would never betray this to Kim. She respected Kim's way of living, even though Lilly, who had never been outside Europe, must have felt it was dangerous. Between Kim's visits in Trelleborg, she kept in touch with her grandmother through postcards and the photographs she sent to us by email with instructions to print them out for Lilly. There were also small presents in her baggage—a small box, an origami bird, a papier-mâché Easter egg.

Kim was so sad when she got the news about her grandmother's death. Now the final tie to the ancestors was broken. Kim had once said, both to Mormor and to us, that if she ever had a daughter, she would name her Lilly. Not only because it was Mormor's name, but because it was beautiful. Mormor scoffed because she didn't think Lilly was a beautiful name at all, and she was completely convinced that it would never again be in style to give it to babies. As it turned out, my usually wise mother was wrong. Today, Lilly is one of the ten most common names in Sweden.

CHAPTER 24

Saturday, November 18, 2017

It's now been one hundred days since Kim went on board the submarine at Refshale Island in Copenhagen. One hundred days of grief and distress and way too many questions that are still begging to be answered. The word *why* has been worn out of our vocabulary.

The weather becomes more important to us this fall than ever before. The winds and waves ought to make the search for the parts of Kim's body impossible to conduct. Even so, we know that the police, divers, and dogs are sailing out onto the November-black water of Öresund in small rubber boats, propelled by the desire to find the rest of Kim's remains. These days are long and, in both senses of the word, dark. We can't do anything—just wait. Wait for a phone call we hope will come, a call that tells us that the search is over—that all of Kim has been found. We know that the conditions are poor—the old, hackneyed phrase about finding a needle in a haystack is relevant, but all too grim in this context.

Sunday, November 19, 2017

Wearing sweaters with Kim's peace sign and her heart and hand emojis, and with the text *Remembering Kim Wall*, two of Kim's friends have fought their way to the finish of the Marabana Marathon in Cuba. Jack Williams and William Denselow got in touch a little while ago and asked if they could run in Kim's name. It's one of the finest and most loving things you can do for another human being. For Jack and Will, there was no question about doing it. They ran despite the heat, not for themselves but for Kim's sake. It felt particularly meaningful that the marathon they ran was in Cuba—this is where Kim wrote one of her final stories—"The Weekly Package"—about how people in a totalitarian country find ways to take part in modern culture. Jack's and Will's actions—and their encouragement on social media—got many to donate to Kim's fund.

Sunday, November 26, 2017

Swedish Television has worked on a documentary about Kim this fall. As we have so many times before, we refrain from participating. We've heard from friends, acquaintances, and colleagues that it hasn't been easy to find anyone who will talk about her—the time that has elapsed since the catastrophe is too short. We are asked if we can contribute with video footage from Kim's childhood. We hesitate at first, but then decide to look in our enormous archive. We set conditions for how the material may be used, and, most important, royalties must be paid as for any other copyrighted material. Not for us—not one crown—the money will go to the fund. Good journalism costs money, and if we don't protect it, who will?

A few days before the broadcast, we drive to the TV building in Malmö to see the thirty-minute documentary. We understand that it wasn't easy to make—journalists have feelings just like anyone else—and in this case, the subject is a colleague who's died on assignment. We also don't know how we ourselves will react since it's the first time we're seeing a program of this type. How have the journalists approached this sensitive material? As it turns out, they've done a very good job of respectfully creating a portrait of Kim.

We watch, we cry, we laugh. We get an explanation for the photos of feet wearing tennis shoes on Kim's laptop. She and her colleague and friend Yan Cong bought shoes at the same time in Beijing—they are their reporter shoes. The girls exchanged photos of their shoes with each other, taken when they were out on assignments all over the world. The white cloth shoes became their own gimmick—a way of saying hello to each other from different parts of the globe. Kim was wearing her white shoes when she climbed up in the tower on the *Nautilus* on August 10. The shoes were found two months later—in a plastic bag weighted down with pieces of metal.

The trailer for the program is shown constantly the week before the broadcast.

Few people, if anyone, can have missed the program about Kim—*The Woman Who Wanted to Tell Stories.* That Sunday evening, many took a seat in front of the television in order to get a picture of the woman who dominated the news during the late summer and fall. During the days that followed the program, we got many comments from people. The program had moved them, and for the first time they felt they had gotten to know Kim the person—not Kim the victim.

CHAPTER 25

In the fall of 2014, Kim decides to embark on a big adventure with two friends and schoolmates from J-School, Jan Hendrik Hinzel and Coleen Jose. The trio wants to tell the story of how American atomic bomb testing is continuing to destroy the environment as well as ruining the living conditions of the people on the Marshall Islands in the Pacific. The Marshall Islands is one of the world's smallest nations, with a population the size of a medium-sized Swedish city—just over 53,000 people. Over hundreds of years, the islands were colonized by a succession of rulers. In 1979, the Marshall Islands became an independent republic, and in 1983, the island nation signed an agreement with the United States. It is essentially entirely dependent on the US for support.

To the rest of the world, the Marshall Islands are best known as the place where the US conducted a long series of atomic bomb tests during the years following World War II. The coral atoll Bikini even gave its name to the two-part bathing suit. The other atoll, Enewetak, is not as well known, but this is where Kim and her friends traveled during the late spring of 2015.

The islands consist of coral chalk and sand, and are hit regularly by hurricanes and floods. Since no point on the islands is higher than twenty feet, it is easy to imagine the kinds of damage nature can wreak there. As a consequence of the atomic bomb testing, the population of the Marshall Islands have become nuclear nomads. Test bomb Castle Bravo, detonated in 1954, was at least one thousand times stronger than the Hiroshima bomb and forced them to leave their islands. The population was evacuated to other islands in the atolls—temporarily, it was said—but as it turned out, their original islands were contaminated. Tests showed that people here had received the largest dose of plutonium that had ever been measured in a population. Now yet another threat has joined the others—climate change has made the sea level rise, and there's a risk that the atomic waste in the atolls will leak out into the ocean. Kim, Coleen, and Hendrik come to the Pacific very well prepared. On Christmas Day 2014, they go to Arkansas to meet some of the people who were forced to flee their home country as a result of the American bomb testing. They interview and listen. And then they go to the Marshall Islands to see for themselves the state of the people and the environment.

The three journalists—one writing, one taking pictures, one taking videos—arrive in the capital Majuro during late winter 2015. From here, they travel farther by boat. They've booked passage on the ship *Lady E*, which regularly provides food and other necessities to the remote islands. The bomb testing has meant that fishing in the water or growing food in the sparse earth isn't possible—everything is contaminated. For Kim and her colleagues, the encounter with the Marshall Islands is an exercise in patience. Day after day, new excuses are made for why the ship can't leave. The boat is small, the ocean is huge, and on board there are both people and animals that will sail over the Pacific, a trip lasting several days. This is how Kim herself describes the long wait through what she calls a list of excuses why *Lady E* still hasn't left the harbor:

> *Tuesday: Lady E "isn't ready yet"—day of departure is withdrawn without any details given.*

Friday: D-day—the ship's engineer has quit, no known rea-
son. Day of departure postponed to Saturday.

Saturday: D-day again! When a new engineer was flown
in, it was discovered that a replacement compressor has
disappeared—with rumors of corruption and safety measures
that are being ignored. Day of departure postponed to Sunday;
the passengers spend their first night on board.

Sunday: D-day, this time for real. The replacement compressor
was found, but suddenly a new generator is needed, and the
hardware store is closed.

Day of departure moved to Monday, maybe.

Pack, unpack, pack again—we're continuing to sleep on board, writes
Kim in an email to us. Finally, they are off. The reportage that the three
friends deliver isn't just incredibly informative and well done—it's also
extremely important. People living on canned goods—on islands that,
on the surface, look like they're taken from a travel brochure from
paradise—deserve to have their voices heard. Kim listens, writes, and
publishes. She, Hendrik, and Coleen make a difference; the stories of
the Marshall Islands people are spread all over the world. The reports
are published in leading papers in Germany, Italy, and other countries.
The trio is also awarded a prestigious prize one year later: Germany's
Hansel-Mieth-Preis.

The trip to and around the Pacific—which lasts several months—is
not without its dangers. Besides the voyage on the small boat across the
ocean, there is the disconcerting possibility that the journalists have
been exposed to radiation, particularly when they visit the large con-
crete dome that was built on top of the radioactive debris left over from
the tests. The trio has Geiger counters with them, and before they leave

the island, they are in isolation for twenty-four hours, allowed to eat and drink only strictly controlled food. Their readings are taken both before and after, and then a very long wait begins for the results. It will be an entire year before these are available.

Meanwhile, Kim becomes worried about what might have gotten into her system. One way of tackling this fear was to find a neon sign that said "ATOM"—a sign that had the place of honor in the apartment in Williamsburg. Along with the sign, the trip to the islands has given Kim many stories. They had met a couple who had once worked as rocket specialists for Muammar al-Qaddafi. The woman was of German extraction and was the goddaughter of one of the highest leaders in Nazi Germany. In their living room, the couple—who lived as nudists on their own island—had hung a still life with flowers painted by Adolf Hitler.

The trip to the South Pacific has given Kim a taste for more. On board the *Lady E*, Kim writes an application for a fellowship from Foreign Policy Interrupted, an organization whose goal is to increase the number of women's voices in foreign policy. She wants to learn more about foreign reporting and writes this about herself:

> *I'm writing this from a supply ship owned by the government of the Marshall Islands. We're somewhere in the middle of the northern Pacific. I'm sitting on the bridge, looking out over the ocean and the old-fashioned navigation instruments and hoping I'll reach land—and Wi-Fi—before the deadline.*
>
> *It's our fifth day on board, and we're already delayed one day. Just now I'm on my first large assignment, a multi-media reportage series about climate change and a constantly present nuclear weapon "inheritance" on the Marshall Islands. I've spent the last few months researching American policy on this small island nation.*

Kim goes on to tell about the trio's ambitions for telling stories in a new way, using modern technology such as drone photos, videos, and sound recordings. The effect is meant to strengthen the message.

> *I've always been attracted to opposites. With my background in postcolonial and feminist interpretations of international affairs during my baccalaureate years at the London School of Economics, I've found that odd stories have become a theme in my work. I entered the field of foreign policy first from the diplomatic side since I worked for the Swedish Foreign Office and the European Union in Australia and India. I was frustrated by having to summarize important stories into short policy sketches, often sent to decision makers in encrypted form. I want my writing to result in something else: getting people involved and maybe affecting policy from the grass roots up, not the other way around.*

CHAPTER 26

December 2017

Will it never end? We thought that interest in the so-called submarine case would diminish after a few months. At the end of November, Kim's arms are found. First the left, then the right—her writing arm. By then, 111 long days have passed. As have 111 even longer nights.

Finally, all of Kim's body has been retrieved from the sea. It's a feeling of closure, but at the same time it means that we have to think about the truly difficult part: the funeral. In some way, we've pushed the thought of a burial ahead of us as we've waited for Kim to become "whole" again. Insensitive journalists have already asked the question several times, but they haven't gotten an answer. On the one hand, we don't have an answer yet; on the other hand, this is a private issue. Kim's funeral, whenever it happens, will not become a media event.

Is there anything left for the reporters to write about until the trial next year? Maybe we can downshift a little, stop seeing headlines and pictures everywhere, have time to think, to catch up. To breathe! But we don't get a chance.

The smallest piece of non-news becomes news when there's nothing to write about. A postponed detention hearing, a charge that hasn't been submitted, how the prisoners in Vestre Fængsel spend their Christmas Eve. According to tradition, a list of words and concepts that have been Googled the most by the Swedish people is published the last week before Christmas. Not surprisingly, Kim's name is high up on the list. And the same thing happens in Denmark. New headlines, new pictures. Soon the year-end chronicles will be broadcast, and then it's time again. Everywhere we're met by pictures of Kim—she's at the top of the news all over the world. Now the entire year is about to be reported, and the whole story is dragged up again. And again. During the first two months, 44,000 articles were written about Kim in hundreds of papers all over the world. Her portrait has been printed millions of times. Now two more months have passed, and we can estimate that her name and picture have been the subject of around 60,000 articles. She is absolutely the best known Swede of 2017, a title we would happily have seen her without. It seems that the world has an insatiable need for news about Kim and her fate. Some try to make money from it; others have a journalistic interest in providing information. We receive one proposal after another from actors in the industry to participate in documentaries of different types. Don't we want to make sure that the right image of our daughter is projected? At this point, we've repeated our answer so many times that even the most jaded editors begin to understand—the Wall family does not want to participate; we don't have anything to say that hasn't already been said.

One Danish paper makes up a headline: "Wall Family Doesn't Want to Bury Kim." In the same article—which is behind a paywall and thus isn't read by many—it says that the church is ready for the funeral. This is pure speculation, endless guesses and assumptions. A funeral is a private issue, not a spectacle for television cameras. Even the most sensationalist rag should be able to respect a matter like this.

But another picture of Kim is also developing. She is mentioned in an increasing number of contexts, and she's mentioned with respect. The entire fall we've noticed that she's called by most sources "the journalist Kim Wall." I'm not sure another career field would have received such respectful treatment. For us, it's a sign that Kim was one of us, a journalist, one of the gang, one who was hit by the worst possible thing that can happen to a reporter while on duty. We visit the Swedish Publicists' Association in Gothenburg, where we've been invited to talk about the Kim Wall Memorial Fund and to accept a grant in Kim's name. We've consistently said no to all forms of interview about Kim's death this entire time, but the fund—which is so close to our hearts—is something we can talk about all day. It ends up being a very pleasant evening, and we're surrounded by warmth from one-time colleagues and other invited guests. We go home with the knowledge that we've spread a little more information about the legacy we want for Kim.

All through December, money keeps flowing into the fund. *HD-Sydsvenskan*, one of the largest newspapers in the country, gives its entire Christmas donation, 100,000 Swedish kronor—more than 10,000 US dollars—to the fund. "An easy decision," says the editor in chief, "because we want to help make a difference."

Journalism clubs and associations put money into the fund as well as Rotary and Lions clubs. Many private individuals—people we know and complete strangers—show their solidarity with us by contributing. The fact that we are not alone warms our hearts. Almost two thousand people believe that what we are doing is important. For us, it's simply survival—we aren't going to let our Kim be reduced to a victim in a notorious criminal case. Her memory will live on and make an impression. Her tragic death will be given some kind of meaning by allowing other young female journalists to go out into the world and write the stories that Kim wasn't allowed to write.

December is usually the month you write Christmas cards. For more than forty years, we've made our own Christmas cards in which we describe what's happened during the year. Instead, this year we write thank-you notes to people who have supported us in different ways. We've chosen the picture of Kim where she's smiling into the camera, but the numbers at the side of her picture are so hard to look at: 1987–2017.

CHAPTER 27

In May 2015, I had the pleasure of listening to the many different experiences Kim had during her weeks in the Pacific Ocean. It's time for her second graduation at Columbia University. Kim has already finished her studies, of course, just before Christmas—six months ago—but the ceremony only takes place once a year. This time I make the trip over the Atlantic alone. A month before, Jocke had hip replacement surgery, and he can't handle the long flight. I land late in the evening, but as so many times before, Kim is waiting there for me. I go to sleep in Kim's bedroom, in her bed. It's a large, bright room, comfortable to spend time in, with its lush plants in the windows and inviting décor.

This second graduation isn't at all as important to Kim as the one she had two years earlier. Her studies at SIPA haven't fascinated her the same way her journalism classes had.

This trip, more time is spent relaxing. A table is booked at a restaurant. I look around and realize that we have representatives from a large part of the world sitting here—students and parents from Iceland, Norway, and Sweden make up the Nordic delegation; India and Australia for Asia and Oceania; US for the host country. Kim is happy and satisfied that she can check off one more thing on her to-do list. Finally, she is finished with school—fleeting thoughts about pursuing a doctorate are shoved deep in the back of her mind. Now life is going to begin—for real!

Whenever you spent time with Kim, you had a full schedule. Our week in New York is no exception. She was something of an optimist when it came to time and always believed you could fit in more than what the minutes and hours could actually hold. Of course you could squeeze in a visit to the laundromat before going to see our good friends who live an hour north of Manhattan, right? Especially since it was so she could have clean sheets on the bed for the subletters who would stay in the apartment when Kim went back to China.

Howie and Kevin, our longtime friends, have followed Kim ever since she was born. Now we're on our way north along the Hudson River in the beautiful spring sunshine to visit "the uncles." It's a fantastic train ride where the track follows right along the edge of the water. The conductor looks like he's just stepped out of an American film, with a peaked cap and all the rest. The evening ends up being very special. Kim entertains us for hours with her stories, most of them from the Marshall Islands. It almost feels like we're there in the South Pacific instead of sitting at a table in upstate New York. The last time we visited Kevin and Howie together, Kim had just graduated from Columbia the first time. The uncles wanted to celebrate it with a special cake. It was made in the shape of the globe, with all the continents marked on it. The finishing touch was the inscription *The world is yours, Kim!*

On this visit, we also have time for some sightseeing. On the other side of the Hudson, there's a place called Storm King, a gigantic area devoted to outdoor art. We stroll from one work to the next, and make a stop at Zhang Huan's *Three-Legged Buddha*, from 2007. It's made of copper and steel, stretching almost thirty feet into the air. The Buddha's head is pressed down halfway into the ground by one of the three feet.

There's more culture to take in during our days together in New York. There's a Frida Kahlo exhibit at the New York Botanical Garden in the Bronx. Here we're met by a cascade of colors and flowers. In a tasteful way, Kahlo's paintings and life story are interspersed with plants of all kinds. During the week that follows, we also visit a Japanese cat art exhibition and MoMA PS1. As a cat person, Kim loves the former, but she thinks the latter is just plain weird. The video installations aren't worth the trip out to Queens. After we leave the art gallery, we end up at a strange little restaurant where one person does it all—cooks, serves, and entertains the guests. It happens to be the same Saturday that Måns Zelmerlöw wins the Eurovision final, and we follow the voting on our phones with excitement. Under normal circumstances, at home in Sweden, none of us would have cared about it. Now—in the United States—the whole thing becomes a huge deal. The cheers hit the roof in the tiny eatery when it turns out that Måns has won.

This week is also one in which Kim and I have time to talk and be together in a way we haven't done in many years. She shows me parts of New York I've never seen before, and we walk through half of Manhattan to get to a café that has an extremely special cake that Kim has heard about. Once we've found our way there, it turns out that the cake is sold out for the day, but it doesn't matter. The walk through the city is worth the effort.

We take a seat in the small courtyard and enjoy another pastry and a good cup of coffee. And continue to talk—about dreams and hopes, about dreams that never took shape in reality, about future plans and dashed hopes. I get insight into the life Kim is living now, far from my boxed-in existence as a municipal officer in Trelleborg. I'm so proud of Kim—happy that she's so determined and has such a strong will. She doesn't compromise her values even if it's hard sometimes, not least of all financially. Kim knows what she wants, and she plans on getting it, even if there are potholes along the way.

Another day, we're sitting on the big rocks in Central Park and having a lunch of smoothies. As we sit there, we talk about the world, people, and the articles Kim wants to write. I've just read a few novels that are set in Sápmi, formerly Lapland, and tell Kim that I've become fascinated by the conditions of life for humans who don't recognize national boundaries the way we do. We dig deeper into the topic, and she immediately sees the possibilities of telling stories from the perspective of the native people. Is it hard to get there? Can you sell "scoops" that come from there? That afternoon, as my legs fall asleep because of my uncomfortable sitting position, I fully understand Kim's impulse to listen to the small person and give her a voice. She talks about a woman she met on the boat to Enewetak, about her fight to create a tolerable existence for herself and her family—a fight that may turn out to have been in vain.

Kim admired the woman's determination, her bravery, and her stubbornness. However, it didn't occur to her that she showed precisely the same qualities herself.

We leave New York at around the same time. I go home to my everyday life, many memories richer, and happy to have gotten to spend what one calls "quality time" with my adult daughter. We certainly don't agree on everything, but in all the basics we have the same values. On one of the sunny days during my visit, we take the tramway to Roosevelt Island. Oddur takes a picture of the two of us with my cell phone—mother and daughter leaning against the guardrail that separates us from the East River. We smile for the camera. It's one of the few pictures from later years that I have of just us two. These days the cell phone picture—taken on a whim—is the desktop background on my computer.

I fly to Copenhagen, and Kim flies to Oslo a few days later. Once again, a bunch of friends from college at LSE are meeting in a summer house a bit outside the Norwegian capital. There are many pictures from those days. Being able to get together and having time to catch up on what had happened since the last meetings, walks, and meals—Kim was happy to see her old friends again. I'm sure that she regaled them with stories from her trip on the stormy Pacific aboard the *Lady E*.

Kim has yet another reason to travel homeward, besides seeing her friends. After a lot of work, changing lawyers three times, and a whole lot of money, Kim has succeeded in getting a US visa.

"Exceptional skills" is the term used on the visa, which means that Kim is able to stay and work in the country for three years. Americans are good at bureaucracy, and it isn't simply a matter of getting a visa stamped in your passport. First, Kim had to travel to Washington, DC, to apply for a new passport at the Swedish embassy, because her old one was so full of stamps and visas that there was simply no more room for any more. After that, she had to go to Stockholm, Sweden, to have the visa inscribed into her Swedish passport. This has to be done in Stockholm at the American embassy. The fact that it would have been much simpler logistically to get the formalities out of the way in Copenhagen, an hour's train ride from home, doesn't matter to the Americans. It has to be Stockholm.

Kim flies to Stockholm, visits the embassy, turns in her passport, and receives a piece of paper which states that it normally takes seven days before the visa is ready. *No problem,* Kim thinks. She had planned to take a vacation here at home and with friends in Copenhagen and Malmö. The return ticket to the US is ordered anyway, but the date of departure is far off in the future. However, the days go by, and no passport comes. Countless phone calls to the embassy officers only result in the information that it will come when it comes. The date of departure gets closer and closer, arrives, and goes by. Now Kim's attitude is different—still polite, but not as patient. She has lost several hundred dollars on the nonrefundable ticket.

Time is starting to close in. Kim is on her way to Haiti to write about the years following the horrendous earthquake. As part of the preparations, she is to participate in a conference in Maastricht in the Netherlands. The embassy folks are still unmoved. They can't hurry the visa-passport process.

The last straw comes on the same evening Kim is supposed to fly to the Netherlands. The mailbox is still just as empty as on all other days. Now there is only one alternative: to get an emergency passport, valid for one trip. Kim goes to Malmö to apply for such a passport. She has her suitcase with her—her route takes her directly to Copenhagen and Kastrup. At the passport office in Malmö, it turns out they can't give her a passport, although the man sitting at the computer can see that the young woman on the other side of the glass is Kim. She doesn't have any approved Swedish identification! Her driver's license is from the US, and the American ID isn't good enough. Rules must be followed, but if a close relative were to guarantee that Kim is really Kim, they could grant an emergency pass for a rather scandalous amount of money.

Tom throws himself in his car and drives to Kim's rescue. She gets her pink passport document and arrives at her gate in time. This, however, doesn't mean that her worries are over. Would her old permission to enter the US be valid now that she has gotten a permanent visa?

After Holland and an uneasy trip across the Atlantic a few days later, it seems to have worked: Kim gets through the eye of the needle at JFK Airport. The passport drama isn't over, though—we won't be able to take the registered mail slip and pick up her passport since we don't have formal power of attorney. Fortunately, we live on a rural postal route, and other rules apply here. We get the passport, complete with the visa, and send it on to the US. It arrives in time for Kim's first trip to Haiti.

She ends up making two trips to the poor part of Hispaniola that fall. The themes vary, but Kim writes occasionally about Vodou and about how tourism will get the island on its feet after the earthquake. She explores the conditions for migrants who come from Haiti, but who for generations have worked in the Dominican Republic. Both of the countries share the same island, but their inhabitants' quality of life can't be more dissimilar.

In Kim's usual way, she drills down into the stories, goes to see the people, listens, learns, and tells the world. She makes such a strong impression that people from Haiti get in touch after her death, expressing their condolences and wanting to contribute to the fund to honor Kim's memory. They did this despite the fact that they almost completely lacked money for their own existence.

CHAPTER 28

Sunday, December 24, 2017

Christmas comes this year as every other, although it's very different. In previous years, sometimes Kim has celebrated with us and other times she's been far away. However, we've always been able to talk to her by phone and wish each other *God jul*.

Last Christmas we reached her on a static-filled telephone line when she was on a bus from the eastern part of Sri Lanka on her way to the capital, Colombo. She was happy and satisfied, tired and mosquito bitten, but just as perky and merry as usual. The one-month work trip was followed by a few days of relaxation on the beach. Now she was on her way home again—"I'll see you in a few days—we can celebrate Christmas at home, right?" Of course, I reassured her that her Christmas stocking, a bit frayed after following her all the way from elementary school, was still hanging in the usual place, and that we'd saved meatballs and Jansson's Temptation (a traditional potato casserole) for her.

Donald Duck is on the television as usual this Christmas Eve, but Ferdinand the Bull, Cinderella, and the others must present their traditional Christmas stories only to Jocke, Tom, and me—an enthusiastic audience.

The fourth chair is empty—Kim's chair. She would always sit here, with her legs drawn up under her, and talk about all things small and great from the world far away from Gislöv Beach. Despite the empty chair, Kim is with us. Days like this are even harder than all the other difficult days. Just before Christmas, we retrieved a box of her things that a schoolmate had brought home from Beijing. In the box was the camera Kim was so proud of: a Chinese Hasselblad copy with the name Great Wall. She had bought the camera the year before at a market on the outskirts of Beijing. We had told her there was a camera by that name, and together with a colleague, she had gone hunting for a Great Wall. At a visit home, she had shown it to us with great pride. Tom, her photographer brother who also collects cameras, was a little envious that day—he wanted one, too! Kim promised to try to find one for him now that she knew where to look. Now Tom gets his Great Wall camera. It will receive a place of honor in his collection.

Friday, December 29, 2017

Today—Tom's birthday and four and a half months after Kim's death—we receive a notice from the Swedish Tax Agency. She is now registered as deceased. The date of death is August 00, 2017. Nobody—at least nobody who will say—knows what day Kim died, and assumptions have no place in the world of national registration. Two zeros stand in place of the tenth of August.

Sunday, December 31, 2017

It's windy and rainy, the way it always seems to be on New Year's Eve. At midnight, we talk to those closest to us on the phone and decide that 2018 has to be a better year than 2017—an unspeakably bad one. There's a missing phone call: the one that usually comes from Copenhagen, New York, Beijing, or some other part of the world. This call would sometimes last a half hour or so, depending on where in the world Kim was at the time. But it always came—greetings and wishes for a happy new year from a daughter to her parents. During the evening, my cell phone dings. It's Kim's cousin Magnus and his family, on semester in Thailand, sending us a short video clip. It's already midnight in Khao Lak, and on the beach, the family has gathered to send up a burning lantern into the dark sky—a lantern for Kim.

Friday, January 5, 2018

In our family, having a birthday usually doesn't mean any great to-do. Dinner together, if possible. Last year, on my sixty-first birthday, Kim brought me curry and tea from Sri Lanka and an orchid from Copenhagen. This year, we're reminded of her in another almost eerie way. A postal notice arrives for a package that hasn't yet been picked up. We had never seen an original notice, and I wasn't expecting a package, either. It turns out to be Kim's clothing, sent from China a month earlier.

It feels as if Kim wanted to be there for my birthday. But opening the suitcase and going through her clothes feels too heavy—it'll have to wait. Probably a rather long wait, because it hurts so much to go through her clothes. This is—was—Kim. We've seen her in this dress and this sweater.

CHAPTER 29

In the fall of 2015, Trelleborg and Sweden, in general, are marked by the large number of refugees that arrive. Trelleborg is designated the municipality of entry for minors who arrive alone, and during the space of ten weeks, around forty-five hundred children and teenagers end up in the harbor town on the southern Swedish coast. In my work as a communications officer, I work almost around the clock managing the refugee situation. We receive media from both Europe and the US. Kim is on the other side of the Atlantic, but she's following the events on this side. All of a sudden, the world has landed in her sleepy little childhood town. We have frequent contact during the intense weeks when boatload after boatload of young boys, mostly from Afghanistan, arrive in Trelleborg.

When Kim comes home for Christmas, the refugee situation is naturally of the greatest interest to her. Not far from where we live, an old retirement home no longer in use had been put into service as a transitional residence for those arriving in Sweden alone. On Christmas Eve, Kim walks over despite clear warnings from me that no journalists are allowed into the residences. But of course Kim succeeds in talking to some of the young refugees.

In different ways, she continues to work on the story. She visits other facilities as well as the offices of the Swedish Migration Board in

Malmö, and she bombards me with questions: How? Why? Where? The benefits and shortcomings of Sweden's refugee policy is a constant companion of the Wall family that Christmas.

Kim was especially skillful at getting answers, getting me to think things over, to articulate my answers and not simply deliver standard phrases. We also talk a lot about what these young men—and a few women—can have gone through during their travels through Asia and Europe to a small town way up north. We talk about injustice, about being born in the "right" part of the world, how war can change living conditions. We talk at length about how Swedes and other Europeans feel about the people seeking shelter in our countries. About what effect that can have on Swedish society and different parties' policies. At the peak, Trelleborg had more than one thousand young people housed in an old museum, industrial premises, and other empty buildings. We opened seventeen residences in as many days. We had decided that these people would have their most basic needs met: food in their stomachs, a roof over their heads, and a bed to sleep in. A large part of the Swedish public looked the other way and let Trelleborg face the problem alone.

This fall, Kim was proud of me and of Trelleborg, which had succeeded in taking care of those who wanted a temporary home in our midst.

She dug deeper and became involved in a legal case in which two underage refugees arriving together were victim and possible perpetrator.

For Kim, the world shrunk a bit more during these months. It is no longer possible to divide the world into rich and poor, as we've been accustomed to doing for so many centuries. Today, conditions can change, and change rapidly. Then, of course, it's a question of how many refugees a country can take in. The interpretations are many, and certainly diametrically opposed if you see it from a Lebanese or a Swedish perspective.

CHAPTER 30

January 2018

In the new year, Kim's name is still being mentioned in many different contexts. In *Journalisten*, our industry journal, two colleagues designate her as Journalist of the Year for 2017. The OPC, Overseas Press Club of America, launches its new prize for the best digital reporting—the Kim Wall Best Digital Reporting Award. She is in distinguished company—other prizes are named for Robert Capa, Ed Cunningham, and Cornelius Ryan. Kim is probably the first Swedish journalist honored in this way. This is what the organization itself writes in a press release:

> *The Overseas Press Club of America has named its Best Digital Reporting Award in honor of Kim Wall, a Swedish freelance journalist and OPC member who was murdered while working on a story in Denmark in August, 2017 . . . Now the OPC is honoring her legacy with The Kim Wall Best Digital*

Reporting Award for best story or series of stories . . . using
creative and dynamic digital storytelling techniques.

The first Kim Wall Award will be given on April 26 in New
York at the OPC's annual awards dinner. Wall's parents will
attend the dinner and light the OPC's candle of remembrance
in honor of journalists murdered, jailed, or missing.

"The Overseas Press Club is honored to be able to commemo-
rate the life and work of Kim Wall with this award," said
OPC President Deidre Depke. "Kim was a journalist who
embodied the club's commitment to quality journalism and
courage in the field."

Thursday, January 11, 2018

Finally! Today we can start to accept applications for the first grant that
will be distributed by the Kim Wall Memorial Fund. In the middle of
this coal-black tragedy, it feels like we've won a victory—a victory of
love over hate. Together with around two thousand people all over the
world, we've created a fund that will be able to award grants for many,
many years to come. We're close to $150,000—a considerable amount
of money. On Kim's birthday, March 23, the first recipient will be presented with a check for $5,000. The money will be used for a reporting
trip in Kim's spirit—with an amount generous enough to cover respect-
able accommodations and insurance. Soon word will spread all over the
world, and we're waiting eagerly for the first applications. We hope and
believe that the fund will ensure that Kim is remembered as the human
being and journalist she was—not as a person who became the victim
of a violent act on a submarine in Copenhagen.

Friday, January 12, 2018

The big logistics company has left its load in our driveway: 388 pounds of Kim's life. The things we packed up in her apartment at the beginning of October have come home. A large pallet with boxes and suitcases carefully wrapped in black plastic: This is what's left of Kim's years in New York.

Here are all her books. On the top is a guidebook to the Trans-Siberian Railway—a trip that was on her agenda for several years. Here are her beloved Fjällräven jackets, the sweatshirt I bought myself in Greenland in 1990 and which she appropriated because of the text on it: *Kalaallit Nunaat—Land of the People.*

We find clothes, souvenirs, piles of notebooks, pictures of us. It hurts so much—but at the same time, it feels like Kim is sitting on a chair next to us and explaining everything. Here's a kind of medallion of Mao Zedong with a younger version on the front, an older one on the back. Carefully, we lift out the delicate tiger mask she bought in India in connection with the report she made on the poaching of the beautiful animal. Here's the daisy pin we gave her when she graduated in London. She loved this piece of jewelry and wore it every day for several years.

The large boxes contain Kim's collection of North Korean proletarian posters. Here's the portrait of Kim and Oddur. It's a drawing that the friends had done in Beijing a few years ago and that decorated the wall in their apartment in Williamsburg thereafter.

Most important of all, however, is the neon sign with the letters *ATOM* in red that she bought after the months she spent on her report from the Marshall Islands in the South Pacific. Now it will have a place of honor in our home, a symbol of Kim's desire to do the right thing and not avoid what must be done. The story of the cynical exploitation of humans and the environment was more important than her own health. Kim didn't compromise—the story came first.

CHAPTER 31

2016

Kim goes back to New York via Iceland, this time to prepare herself for a new continent: Africa. With the help of the IWMF, she's gotten the opportunity to travel to Uganda. Together with a group of other women journalists, she will report from the African Great Lakes. The trip begins in Kenya, where the whole group participates in a three-day training called HEFAT, Hostile Environment and First Aid Training. The IWMF, which for many years has promoted and fought for the rights of women journalists, has by now given around four hundred reporters training that can be the difference between life and death. Kim was extremely happy, grateful, and full of anticipation before the trip to Kenya and Uganda, and the HEFAT course was one of the reasons.

For three days, Kim and her colleagues were treated to both practical and theoretical training behind the desk and in simulated situations. The course included first aid, digital security, self-defense, personal safety, safety when staying in a hotel, social unrest and demonstrations, kidnappings, reactions during shootings, alertness, and how to handle feelings. Kim was in no way naïve before the course, but this gave her a foundation and knowledge that she was very grateful for. In addition, it gave her lovely memories and a lot of laughs—we've seen pictures from the course showing how serious topics were mixed with mirth. On-site in Uganda, there was no place for laughter. Kim wanted to talk about the dictator Idi Amin's torture chambers. She visited several of them, spoke to next of kin, and produced a frightening documentation of the evil deeds committed against his own people. She didn't rest after this, but found representatives of the Ugandan film industry, Wakaliwood, and ended up not only getting a good story, but acting as an extra (along with her friends) in a movie that was being filmed while they were there. After Uganda, Kim took a trip to Beijing, as she had done so many times before. She had decided to deepen her knowledge of Chinese. In order to be able to speak to people there, and to be able to truly reach them, she needed to learn more. Chinese isn't one single language, but several.

During the winter after her death, when we receive her belongings from New York, there are a number of textbooks and dictionaries in Mandarin. In the spring of 2016, Kim had registered for an intensive course in Mandarin. Every morning she spent several hours with her teacher. It was rather expensive, but Kim saw it as an investment in her future. She was going to live in China at some point, and the language would be her key to success. On this trip to China, she didn't simply take a plane or two. Kim and Oddur decided to fly to China from California, and to get to California by train. They traveled across the entire United States, from the East Coast to the West. It took a few days and was probably rather boring from time to time. On the West Coast, the friends rented a car and experienced California before it was time to fly west across the Pacific to Beijing.

One Monday afternoon in May, my work phone rang. It was Kim, wondering if we were able to come to Berlin at the end of the week. She was about to board a plane in Beijing bound for Munich. We found out that she and her colleagues Hendrik and Coleen were going to receive the Hansel-Mieth-Preis in Germany for their report on the Marshall Islands. We hadn't even known they were nominated, and we were of course ecstatic. We also wanted to grab the opportunity to see our daughter in the flesh. Our calendars were quickly cleared, we were able to find a hotel in Berlin, and we were off on short notice.

Kim and her friends receive the prize in Stuttgart, and on Ascension Day, Jocke and I stand on the platform at Berlin Hauptbahnhof to meet Kim's train. Once again we have a few intense days ahead of us. We stand on a parking structure above a gallery that has been annexed by a group of idealists and transformed into a meeting place for young people. From there we have a splendid view of Berlin. Kim finds a Russian tea salon and climbs up the only remaining guard tower from the days of the Berlin Wall. We visit Tempelhof, an airport no longer in use that has become an oasis for people living in the middle of the bustling metropolis.

On Saturday evening, we drop her off at Tegel Airport. Kim is in a hurry to get back to Beijing—her textbooks were expecting her on Monday morning. We get proof of the importance of her course when she proudly tells us that she was able to converse with a taxi driver in his native language on her way to the airport before her trip to Europe.

A couple of months later, Kim was in Europe again, but this time on an assignment unusual for her—she was observing a sports event, the European Football Championship. Kim was completely uninterested in sports, but the story of how the little island nation of Iceland took the whole world by storm through its progress in the tournament—she couldn't miss that. Together with half-Icelanders Oddur and Vidar, she enjoyed David's struggle against Goliath. This story had everything Kim stood for: a small challenger dismissed beforehand, a challenger who shows a strong will and succeeds.

After soccer in Europe, it was Cuba in the Caribbean. Among other things, Kim was going to do research for a larger article planned for late September and early October. She spent most of the late summer in Copenhagen. We began to suspect that there was something special that drew her to Denmark, but, as usual, Kim didn't say much about why she was there. It would take several months before we found out that the reason was spelled O-L-E.

Kim was supposed to depart on her second trip to Cuba from Copenhagen, but there were several obstacles in her way. When she arrived at Kastrup, the airline refused to seat her although she had a valid ticket. One document was missing—a document she hadn't needed on her previous trip a little over a month before. People were waiting for Kim in Cuba, and she felt she had to get there. She tried to buy a new ticket, but her credit card gave her trouble in the middle of the night, and she didn't get one. Waiting for the morning wasn't an option for Kim, but thanks to Ole in Copenhagen, attempt number three was successful, and now she was on her way.

A few days later, we got a call in the middle of the night. Kim didn't feel safe where she was staying, and she wanted to go to a better place. Now. Immediately. Could we possibly send her some money? Of course we could, and Kim moved to safe ground. Fresh in her memory was a mugging in Havana during her visit in July. In the middle of the street, in broad daylight, her valuables, phone, and bank cards were stolen.

Her visit to Cuba in September resulted in an article published in the monthly *Harper's Magazine*. Kim writes about "the weekly package" (*el paquete*), which is how people who live isolated from the internet and the Western news flood can stay updated, thanks to subversive activity.

CHAPTER 32

Monday, January 15, 2018

A gray, windy day in January, a month in which there isn't usually much joy, and in our situation, there's an even larger distance between the points of light. However, a small candle is lit when we find out that the Kim Wall Memorial Fund has reached over $150,000. Through her fund, Kim will do what children are supposed to do: outlive their parents. This comforts us in our grief. More comments from supporters on why they are donating money to Kim's fund:

> *May Kim's memory shine forever.*

> *No words can describe the pain.*

> *May God protect the journalists that seek the truth despite the dreadful terrors they meet in this brutal world.*

Help for those who follow in Kim's footsteps.

An honor to be able to contribute.

Journalists are the last defense against totalitarianism.

Kim and those like her are my heroes.

CHAPTER 33

Tuesday, January 16, 2018

One more day that I'd like to erase from the calendar. We've been asked to come to Copenhagen to be informed about the main elements of the indictment that will be submitted to the court today. On the wall in Jens Møller Jensen's office hang several different kinds of animal horns. Spending time in nature, fishing, and hunting must be activities that give him relief from what is no doubt a stressful, pressure-filled work life. Now, another kind of hunt is entering its final phase. Jens methodically goes through the different points in the charges, which are being explained to the defendant at the same time in a jail in another part of the city. Jens answers all our many questions patiently, and gives us an idea of how the trial will progress. We also find out what sentence the prosecutor will request: life in jail or custody. The Danish term *custody* means a sentence without a specific time limit that can be pronounced on a person who is considered dangerous to society.

Ten, twelve, fourteen, or more years. This doesn't help us. We'll never get our Kim back.

But now justice will be served. We don't know what happened down there in the depths of Öresund; we don't know if the trial will provide us with any answers. Lies have followed lies during the past five-plus months. Will the defendant talk in the courtroom, and if so, can we believe what he's saying? The trial will begin on International Women's Day, March 8. Maybe it's a coincidence, or maybe a twist of fate. One message we receive today makes us relieved, if not happy. We've imagined a scenario in which someone with a strange moral compass buys the submarine—buys it in order to put it on display, for the hype. There are probably people out there who would pay to go on board the submarine where our daughter died. We express our misgivings, and apparently there are others who have seen the same risks. The indictment includes forfeit and destruction of the submarine. If the court shares our opinion, the black vessel will disappear forever, and then we won't have to see it show up at some amusement park. I've thought a lot about the earrings Kim was wearing the last time she was at home. Now we've gotten them back in a neat Ziploc bag—I had to sign for them on an official form. It seems odd to hold the bag in my hand. I can see Kim with the thin, vertical metal bars in her ears. I can see them lying on the windowsill in the bathroom. I refuse, however, to take in the image of these simple pieces of jewelry lying on the bottom of the sea for almost two months, still serving as an adornment for their owner.

We also receive word that the prosecutor will hold a brief press conference in the afternoon, a couple of hours after the press release is made public. We find out what the press release says and can guess the magnitude of media interest. As we suspected, it doesn't take long before the press hunts us down—our answer, as always, is that we have nothing to say. And that would be true even if we wanted to say something. What do you say when your daughter has been attacked and killed in such a brutal way? There's no instruction manual for parents whose child has been murdered. Somehow, this day ends—many news reports and updates later. Now we simply need to prepare ourselves mentally. In one week, the media will have access to the entire indictment and then, in all likelihood, more information will be released.

Sunday, January 21, 2018

It's a wonderful Sunday. The sun is shining, and you can almost feel spring in the air. The snowdrops already bloomed a few weeks ago; here in Scania, the winters are usually without much snow. When we take our morning walk along the beach, Jocke collects more stones, which we'll add to the pile that's been growing a bit above the sandy shore. We think that Ulla, the woman who made the first stone heart, might want to honor Kim with a new one, placed at a more permanent site.

A few hours later, while I'm on my afternoon walk with Iso—now in the grayest fog imaginable—I see the beautifully made heart. I burst into tears—the stone heart has become an important place for us. We pass it several times a day: This is Kim's heart. A simple symbol, a simple act, but so incredibly important for us.

Monday, January 22, 2018

Danish TV 2 has produced a documentary about Kim and the submarine case. The team of reporters worked all fall on it and, just as Swedish Television had done some months ago, tried in different ways to get us and Kim's friends to work with them. As always, we said no—we can't and don't want to say anything. And as we did with Swedish Television and their documentary, we agreed to share material from Kim's childhood—with the condition that it be remunerated in the customary way, and that the money go to the fund. We've been given the opportunity to go to Copenhagen to preview the program.

We sit down on the striped sofa at Danish TV 2's new studios with some trepidation. We know that the reporter was in China, and we know that he was along on a boat to follow the search for the parts of Kim's body. Now we meet him for the first time face-to-face. Quickly, we realize that the chemistry works. Apparently, he's also been worried about meeting us, but our conversation flows easily, and as journalism professionals, we have a lot in common. A few months later we accept the offer from TV 2 to talk about the fund in a separate television program.

Here we'll have the opportunity to talk about Kim and explain what we wish to achieve by supporting other journalists out in the world.

The program proves to be a good, well-balanced documentary where the focus is on the story itself, beginning with the Swedish police dogs—they were so important in locating and salvaging the parts of Kim's body. As dog owners, we're happy to see the fellowship and trust that mark the cooperation between dog and guide. No matter how rough the weather, how high the waves, how cold the temperature, and how difficult the circumstances, two-legged as well as four-legged police have worked tirelessly on the ocean to give us answers. It would also take a while before their efforts bore fruit—it wasn't until the end of August that the first remains were found. They continued to search until the end of November, when the search was finally ended. There were many long, cold hours, but they never gave up. We will always be thankful to them for that.

The program also allows us to see—for the very first time—Kim's home in Beijing and the café where she spent so much time working. We get to meet her colleague Matjaz, who describes Kim as her "soul mate" and who says they were going to conquer the world with their many journalistic projects. "I can't understand that she's dead," Matjaz says, "and the way she died is completely incomprehensible to me."

CHAPTER 34

Back in the US, Kim worked hard on her Cuba story. She also had time for a visit from Ole, who we now knew existed, but who up to this point still had no name. Her American friends knew him as "The Dane" and we knew no more than they did. In early November, elections took place in America—the results of which few could have predicted. I was in Stockholm at a conference, and Kim was in New York at an election watch for Republican women. We kept in contact throughout the night, and we were both forced to realize that what couldn't have happened was actually happening. Kim didn't often work for Swedish media, but this time she was reporting on the election watch for Sweden's Radio P1. As all news journalists are supposed to be, Kim was politically neutral while at work, but her disappointment after the election was something she could discuss with us and with her friends: "I may as well move to China—I won't be able to sell anything in the US anymore, because it will all be about Trump."

Nevertheless, she went to Sri Lanka, not China, after the postelection debates had wound down.

Together with Mansi, a good friend from both J-School and the Uganda trip, Kim has new articles about the aftermath of the civil war on her agenda. For several weeks, Kim and Mansi travel around the northern part of the island. They meet and interview women who had fought for the Tamil Tigers in what they called a war of liberation. We get to hear frightening testimony in the taped interviews. No other army has had so many women in uniform. Their tales are heartrending and grim, but at the same time deeply human. Kim spends Christmas week with another good journalist friend and colleague, May, in Sri Lanka. Their plan is to relax, but they also have conversations about life and the future. The day before they take the bus across the entire island to Colombo for the flights home to Sweden and the US, they perform a local custom: smashing coconuts to dispel evil.

Kim comes home to us to celebrate Christmas 2016, a few days late. Now the veil of mystery around her beloved is lifted: His name is Ole, and Kim speaks of him and their relationship tenderly. Meanwhile, she thinks it's too early for us to meet him. Although they've known each other for a while, their love is so new that it may not survive a visit to any future in-laws. That's what Kim thinks, anyway. Kim divides the winter and spring between Denmark and the US. She celebrates her thirtieth birthday on March 23 in Copenhagen, and we get to see her the day before. We meet in Malmö at a small restaurant Kim has chosen in Gamla Väster.

She's in good spirits, happy, and talks about Ole, about China, and about the future. Soon she's on her way to China again. She has several articles in the pipeline, and she speaks warmly of the old building, a *siheyuan*, that she and Ole will rent in Beijing. In Copenhagen, they live in a room in a collective on Refshale Island. The building once housed a swimming pool facility for the Burmeister & Wain shipyard, and it's now intended to be rehearsal space for musicians, not apartments. But this doesn't bother Kim—she's happy living with her Ole.

Kim visits us on Easter. It's cold and windy, but spring is in the air. Two of Tom's art photos are on exhibit during the Konstrundan art event, and we take Kim there to look at them. It doesn't take long before she's deep in conversation with the art society's chairman about the world and art, and the cultural conditions in China. Kim knows a lot about many things, and she's curious about almost everything. In addition, she's a proud big sister. After seeing the exhibit, we drive a few miles to the northeast on a small country road. I know that there's a great spot for gathering wild garlic next to the old dance hall Grönalund—this green gold that smells and tastes so divine. Kim fills bag after bag with wild garlic and, at the same time, talks about everything that can be made from it—pesto is high on her list. I can still see her before me as she walks through the forest, completely surrounded by wild garlic. Once we're back home, the hunt continues—this time for a recipe for wild garlic pesto. She finds one in a minute or two through the help of Google.

The problem is that the recipe includes cheese. No problem, I say, and offer her a piece of Västerbotten cheese. Well, the problem is that the rest of the people in the collective are vegan, and it's strictly prohibited to have anything nonvegan in the refrigerator. It's unclear how Kim solved this problem—she didn't want to say. But what is clear is that the pesto was truly delicious, *with* Västerbotten cheese.

CHAPTER 35

Tuesday, January 23, 2018

As we wake up, we already know that this is going to be a dreadful day. At lunchtime, the indictment will be made available to the press. We know the main contents, and we know what's going to make headlines and become breaking news. Now the public will also find out that Kim, according to the indictment, was tied up in the submarine. It isn't long before the news has spread all over the world. Radio stations, TV channels, and newspapers report the story. We wouldn't have been able to avoid all this even if we had wanted to. By the afternoon, 466 new articles have been written about the case in all parts of the globe.

As a counterweight to the brutal descriptions, on the same day we've told media in western Europe and the US that the Kim Wall Memorial Fund has now reached over $150,000. Many of the larger media are interested and publish articles on that—this helps a little.

End of January 2018

Several times this winter, we've received proof in different ways about how deeply Kim's fate has affected people—not just in Sweden and Denmark, but elsewhere in the world. In Denmark, many are very upset when a publisher starts to sell a series of e-books that claim to tell about the submarine incident in chapter after chapter. There's a storm of protest, above all on social media, and the company decides to stop publication. There's probably too much goodwill to be lost, but they hedge by saying that it may be more appropriate later on, after the trial.

A few weeks later, many criticize a Danish author who, in an interview with a magazine mostly for women, talks about Kim. He's never met her, but given the image of her that's been spread all over the world, he can see that she's a woman who looks for danger. He may have been implying that the one who plays with fire is going to get burned. Now the Danes rise up once again, and the criticism against the author is merciless. In one of the leading Danish newspapers, one columnist says, among other things, that the world needs more Kim Walls. The author retracts his statement and probably understands that his view of women belongs to another century. I ought to feel rage at this attack on my daughter—I don't think he would have said the same thing if the victim had been a man—but I have no energy for that. Others will have to fight that fight.

CHAPTER 36

Thursday, February 1, 2018

We fly to London to participate in a memorial service for Kim on Friday in the Swedish Church. Kim's friends in London have arranged this event—both schoolmates from the London School of Economics and friends from Columbia University now working in Great Britain. During our days in London, memories come back to us—memories from all the times we were in the British capital with Kim. The first time, she was only a few months old. It wasn't easy wrestling the blue-and-white-striped baby carriage into the black taxi. When she was a teenager, we did the classic tourist things like visiting Madame Tussauds and the Tower of London. The roles were swapped when we traveled to London during Kim's college years. Now she was the one guiding us around "her" city. Kim knew the small restaurants with good food at reasonable prices, knew which market was the best, and took us to Fleet River Bakery, where she had a part-time job. There's so much we would have liked to talk about with Kim. What did she think about England's prospects after Brexit? Will the exit be a serious threat to the EU, or will it strengthen the union? Kim would have had answers—she was always well informed. Now these question marks will have to hang in the air.

The ceremony in the Swedish Church is beautiful, moving, and incredibly sorrowful. Priest Kristina has been preparing herself since November, when the English friends decided to have a memorial service. A young woman herself, she was affected by the tragedy. All of Kim's friends have been—those who, like us, have traveled from Scandinavia as well as those who've come from other parts of England to honor Kim's memory.

Five of us will speak, and I'm the first. Halfway through my script, my voice won't carry anymore. Jocke has to take over and read the rest. It feels surreal to stand in a church in London talking about my dead daughter. It's not right, and it hurts so much. So much. Somehow, however, the words come out anyway and reach everyone in the nearly full church:

> *Paris, London, Hong Kong, New Delhi, New York, Beijing. For the past ten years, our Kim has basically been on the go. She's often been on her way from one place in the world to another. She liked it that way—that's how she lived her life— Kim felt at home no matter where she was, whether there for a short time or a longer stay. No matter where she was in the world, she kept in touch with us here at home base.*

> *Days, even weeks, could go by between signs of life from her, but at least we knew approximately where she was. Soon an email or phone call would arrive. Now we don't know where she is. We only know that we won't hear her voice over a static-filled phone line ever again, or read an email asking us how we are. It's still impossible to take in the extent of the catastrophe that's hit not only us but also friends all over the*

world. Kim loved words, and the word became her weapon
in the fight to create a better world. Now the words have
run out—both for Kim and for us. We don't know what to
say—there aren't enough words for it. Kim, we needed you for
a much, much longer time.

Afterward, it's Ole's turn. He tells three anecdotes about Kim and her phobia of snakes and worms. It's a great relief to be able to laugh while he describes her character so well. Despite her fear of these animals, she respected them and their right to live.

There are many happy memories that are told on this Friday afternoon in February. In the middle of the ceremony, the sun begins to shine through one of the beautiful windows. Maybe we can see it as a sign? We want to see the light and life, not the darkness and death. It's become a kind of mantra for us—to find the points of light in the darkest dark. The rays of the sun help us. I cry as we light candles for Kim.

The line behind us is long—Kim is in everyone's thoughts. While we light our candles, the organist plays two songs that we have chosen—two songs that are Kim. Both "Isabelle" and "Song for Freedom" were written by Björn Afzelius, and both songs personify her.

In the fellowship hall, freshly baked Swedish cinnamon rolls, Swedish coffee, and pictures of Kim are ready. We've put together photos and videos, and so have many of her friends. There is more laughter and more happy memories. Many want to talk to us about their relationship to Kim, how she'd inspired them to make certain choices in life, what she meant to them. For us, it's lovely to hear what an impression she's made on others. We share the joy of having had Kim in our lives, and we share the grief of having lost her. When we come home late Monday night, we're exhausted, but full of thoughts of what fantastic people there are on this planet, people who for a longer or shorter time shared Kim's path on earth.

CHAPTER 37

Saturday, February 10, 2018

It's now been six months since Kim went on board the *UC3 Nautilus*. It's been six months so full of the darkest, blackest despair that it shouldn't have been possible to stand upright and continue to live. At the same time, it's been six months in which we've experienced so much love and warmth that didn't exist in our consciousness before the tragedy struck. We're often asked how we can go on. How are you able to go to work, to perform your daily activities, to function? There's only one answer: We have to. There's no option. Our dog has to go out at least three times a day. We have to make dinner and run the vacuum cleaner once in a while. We have to pay our bills, go to the dentist, and roll the garbage can out to the street when it's our collection day. Everything takes on a different significance for us. What was important before is suddenly completely uninteresting. What does it matter if the windows are clean or if the car's been washed? To be honest, these weren't exactly priorities for us before, either, but now we feel justified in ignoring them. Living with a sorrow so deep and heavy is hard.

Suddenly, without notice, it hits. What seems like a trivial matter can trigger a flood of tears. A memory that suddenly comes to mind can make the world stand still. Sometimes these memories are painful; sometimes they make us smile. We often say to each other that Kim would have liked this, or, conversely, Kim would not have appreciated that. She always tried to get us to be better—get more exercise, buy more organic vegetables, organize the closets, don't drink that glass of wine or eat that red meat. She did this in a very well-meaning way—she wanted us to live a long, long time.

Six months. Sometimes it feels as if the catastrophe happened yesterday; sometimes it's as if we've lived with this grief for a long time. The fact that Kim hasn't sat at our dining room table for six months isn't necessarily an odd thing—she could be abroad for that long. But six months without contact is something we've never experienced. I catch myself waiting for that phone call or the ding from Messenger. There's so much I want to talk to Kim about—hear what she thinks, find out the latest from her. That's probably what hurts the most: I'll never get to talk to her again. Never hear her voice again, her laughter, her opinions about issues great and small. Never need to help her book a flight or transfer money when a credit card acts up. Never again be scolded because the cream cheese in the refrigerator expired two weeks ago.

They say you can learn to live with grief.

Maybe you can—time will tell. We've experienced grief before, of course. We've had parents die and pets who've gone over the rainbow bridge. In those cases, it's a grief you can anticipate, one you know you're going to experience someday. Old people leave an empty place behind them, but there's often a new generation to take over. Pets are beings you really only borrow; you know the day will come when you have to make that awful decision. But a child! A child isn't supposed to die before its parents. A child isn't supposed to fall prey to a brutal act of violence that is completely unfathomable in its cruelty. How can a human being possibly perform the kind of acts that Kim was forced to endure? Kim is in our thoughts around the clock. I haven't slept through the night since we heard that she had disappeared. Every night around 2:00 or 3:00 a.m., the demons sink their claws into me mercilessly. Thoughts, theories, facts about what happened are possible to hold at bay during the day, but at night, the brain takes over and plays scenes that no human being wants to see. Some nights, Kim is very alive in my dreams. Sometimes it's little Mumlan with the unruly hair who's playing with her dinosaurs. Other nights, it's the grown woman who helps me pick red currants and gooseberries to make jam. There are also black dreams that can't be described with words. They're way too macabre and horrifying.

At the same time—thank God—I can feel joy. I enjoy seeing the first snowdrops push their way through the earth, signaling that there will be a spring this year, too.

We can laugh at Iso's way of attacking the fresh snow, throwing himself on the lawn and wriggling in it. We can feel pride about Tom's photographs, published in the paper, and we can feel warmth and consideration from good friends.

I love it when the swans come flying over my head, making their characteristic sounds. I'm happy to hear the first birdsong in the morning. My heart swells when I see that someone has brushed the snow off Kim's stone heart on the beach. To put it simply: Life goes on. Despite everything. Anything else would have been completely unthinkable for Kim. For her, there was only one way, and that way was forward. You only move backward when preparing to pounce.

CHAPTER 38

In the spring of 2017, Ole and Kim lived in the collective on Refshale Island in Copenhagen, just a few hundred yards away from the premises of Copenhagen Suborbitals and its neighbor, Peter Madsen. Kim heard about the space race between the two groups. Up until a few years ago, there was only one—Suborbitals—but after a dispute, Peter Madsen left his old friends and started his own lab—the Rocket Madsen Space Lab.

Kim was intrigued by the stories about these enthusiasts who planned to be the first private citizens to go into space in a privately built rocket. The story about the homemade submarine that would serve as a launchpad for the space rocket was certain to have piqued her interest even more.

This was a story that was right up Kim's alley, and she started to collect information and make pitches for the article to different media. Kim met representatives of Suborbitals and tried in vain to make contact with Peter Madsen. She sent emails and text messages to him, but never got a response. Eventually, she found out that the phone number she'd been given was wrong.

The story was put on the back burner awaiting another opportunity. As it was so many times before, this was unpaid work—but this is the way it is for freelancers, and it was nothing Kim was concerned about. She mentioned the Danes who wanted to go up into space to us, and said that they worked just a few buildings away from her and Ole's home.

CHAPTER 39

February 2018

Once again we drive over the Öresund Bridge toward Sluseholmen and the police station on Teglholm Allé in Sydhavnen. The area is newly renovated; it's been transformed from a dilapidated industrial area into modern residential blocks and offices. The police station is discreetly housed in a brick-clad corner building. There's no sign—nothing indicating that police work here. The receptionist greets us with a warm smile and says, "You're here to meet Jens, right?" as soon as we're inside the door. She has our name badges ready. After quite a number of visits, we're well known here. A half minute later, Jens Møller Jensen comes down the stairs and gives us warm handshakes. We first heard about this fifty-eight-year-old police officer with the title *politimester*—chief of police—six months ago, when we learned he was head of the unit that deals with what are called *crimes against persons*.

The term *crimes against persons* sounds frightening, but the impression is softened a bit when we see that the coffee thermos Jens puts on the table in front of us has a label with the same words.

His office is large and full of light; he has a window on what is a parking lot now, but which will probably become yet another apartment building as more and more Danes move to the capital region.

There's an ancient typewriter on a small table and a modern computer on a larger one. A very special poster fills one entire wall. It's a representation of different phenomena in society, and in the middle stands the typical police station in central Copenhagen. The pictures are accompanied by the numbers "007" and "112"—references to James Bond and the European equivalent of 911. It's quite clear that this artwork was painted by a police officer, for his choice of profession is obvious in the images. On the wall behind Jens's desk, there's a bulletin board full of pictures. He shows one photo of the three royal Swedish children, taken at Crown Prince Frederik's wedding a few years ago.

"Someone sent it to the Swedish secret service, who made sure I got it," Jens says proudly and shows that he's the one standing behind the three members of the royal Bernadotte family. "I was in charge of the command at the wedding," he explains. Jocke realizes that he, too, was there observing the same event. Soon they're both involved in a conversation about the work conditions for photographers and police during an event like a crown prince's wedding.

A few days later, Jocke has gone through his old photographs and found Jens in several of them. On that beautiful early summer day in Copenhagen, no one could have imagined that Jens and Jocke would cross paths again in this dreadful way.

As the months have gone by, we've grown to trust Jens Møller Jensen completely. He's calm and secure, and extremely eager to make sure that we find out information from him and not through the media. He had decided already on that very first day to stay in touch with us himself. It would have been so easy to delegate the task to a subordinate, but that's not how Jens thinks. We've had reason to be grateful to him time and again for his great empathy and sensitivity to our situation. At the same time, he has never compromised the confidentiality regulations governing the inquiry phase of the case.

Jens Møller Jensen is a hunted man, and he's been so ever since that Friday morning in August when he decided to arrest Peter Madsen. His phone rings off the hook. He tries to be available to the media, and he stays in touch with his colleagues and the authorities involved in the search for the submarine, Kim, and other objects.

His workdays are long; we can reach him just about any time of day or night, seven days a week. No matter how full his calendar is, he always makes time for us and our questions. This, of course, has had enormous importance for us, because we know there's someone who will listen. We've never experienced anything like this before, but knowing that there's a human being on our side is precious. Even though he is 100 percent professional, we know that the case affects him deeply.

He's investigated many grim criminal cases, but that has hardened him only to some extent.

"Of course you're affected. Otherwise, you wouldn't be a human being," Jens says simply.

It's easy to talk to Jens, and he listens and answers. He gets our need to try to understand what happened. His empathy is real. Had we met under other circumstances, we would have become good friends, no doubt. Now his task is to solve the murder of our daughter, and he's using all his power and all his resources to do so. No stone has been left unturned, all the clues have been followed up on, and all the strange thoughts that pop up into our heads get a response. We haven't felt like we've been a burden at all. Without Jens's patience and empathy, these months would have been even more hellish.

The trust and security we feel with Jens carries over to the press conferences we follow on television as well. We know in advance the most important things he's going to say—what he's already told us—but as journalists, we appreciate his professional demeanor before the TV cameras and microphones. He never loses focus, he says what he's decided he will say, and he does it with dignity and without drama.

Today we're going to get information about how the trial will go as well as a preview of the practical matters involved. Jens draws on his pad: This is where the judge will sit, here's where Madsen and his attorney will be, here's the prosecutor.

Some of the seats are reserved for us, fewer for Madsen's family.

Jens also tells us that several media companies have gotten in touch with the municipality of Copenhagen and want to put up tents outside the courthouse in order to be able to broadcast directly from the trial. Interest is tremendous. There's room for a total of ninety-five journalists in the courtroom and the overflow room that will be arranged. Journalists from twelve different countries have already expressed their interest. We're terrified thinking about the first day of the trial, and we know that we'll be the target of the insatiable appetites of hungry reporters. Everyone will get the same response: We have nothing to say. The trial will begin in a week or so, and we hope that answers will be revealed then. We don't have any—there's only one person who knows what happened in the vessel after it dived under the surface of the ocean in Öresund. Will he talk? And if he does, will we get to hear the truth?

The lack of facts means that many try to embellish available details—in some cases, there's not even a nubbin of truth in what's published. One of Sweden's evening papers succeeds in really hitting bottom. Their first page shouts: "Life of Murder Suspect Madsen in Shambles. Denied Visitors to His Cell. Wife Has Left Him."

What on earth is this for? Are we supposed to feel sorry for this man? Is his life in shambles because he can't have visitors or because his wife wants to divorce him? Not because of what he's accused of? And what about Kim's life? Our lives? In our local supermarket, the cashier wishes she could remove all the newspapers from their rack beside the cash register. This first page makes several people decide not to buy the paper—pity for the perpetrator has the opposite effect. In social media, many air their opinions about the paper, and these opinions are definitely not positive. At this point, though, we're jaded. We've seen so many news banners, seen so many black headlines. Good journalism is mixed with articles of significantly poorer quality. We've also seen how different media view press ethics. It isn't just national characteristics— there's a big difference between various types of media.

We're not like other people. Many who go through the hell we're living in right now decide not to read papers or watch television. To the contrary: We have an occupational habit that makes us look for information. We would probably have felt better if we didn't, but we can't refrain. We've always followed big news stories, and the submarine incident fulfills all the criteria for just such a story. We want to know, but we ourselves refuse to participate in the media circus. We're the only ones who can tell that story, and we'll do it, in our own way, when it's time.

CHAPTER 40

Soon Kim is back in Beijing again. She sends us pictures of where she lives, of her rowing a dragon ship, of the Forbidden City. We'd talked a lot about our upcoming trip to China, planned for the fall. One day the phone rings as I sit working in city hall. "Hi, it's me," the conversation begins. "I'm so tired of noodles that I just biked for an hour and a half to a market where they sell Western food, and now my credit card won't work! Can you put some money on my other card?" What mother can resist such a request? Five minutes later, my cell pings and I get a picture of an overflowing bicycle basket.

These kinds of things happened frequently. It would be quiet for a few days, and then contact with home base was made to get help of some kind. It could be a cinnamon bun recipe, help booking a flight, or a temporary cash infusion. But it could also be a picture of a T-shirt with a misspelled message, or a blossoming cherry tree.

Kim communicated by phone and by computer. Often when she was at home with us, she was tapping frantically on her digital tools. With a cup of coffee or a glass of wine beside her, she stayed in touch with her clients, friends, and colleagues. If you asked her what she was doing, she always answered the same way: "I'm working."

Late nights, early mornings, and all the time in between, we could hear the clicking of her nails against the keyboard or quiet conversations on her cell phone. It didn't matter what time zone it was or where she was in the world—Kim was incredibly careful about staying in touch with her friends. We got to hear about long chats, pictures, and greetings sent here and there across the globe. She almost never forgot a birthday, and she knew what her friends were interested in, what made them happy, what flaws they had. In her typical Kim way, she tried to turn misery into something positive. When one of her friends got divorced, Kim arranged a party to celebrate her escape from an unhappy marriage. When another friend was beaten up, Kim didn't settle for expressing her sympathy. She wanted to have an actual pity party. Finding the silver lining in all clouds was something Kim did to perfection.

She could also find the perfect gift. For Mother's Day a few years ago, she ordered a front page of the *New York Times* from the day I was born. And it was in the form of a jigsaw puzzle. Kim shared my passion for large, difficult puzzles. For my sixtieth birthday, an oblong package came from Uganda. It contained a painting from Uganda created on a background of plant fibers. Two African women are each carrying a jug of water.

The spring months in China go quickly, even more so after Ole comes to keep her company. They travel around the country by train; they find the *siheyuan* where they will live when they return for a year's stay. Kim works on different articles and background information. Kim is happy—it probably feels like she's finally established her reputation firmly enough to be a successful freelance journalist. Or, as she says herself, "The editors are calling me back—they know who I am now."

CHAPTER 41

Early March 2018

We're ready. We know how this theatrical work is structured—we know how the news outlets function. Even so, we're struck by the magnitude of interest on the part of the media when the first day of the trial approaches. It's complete hysteria—a tsunami of inquiries, articles, videos, and everything else that has a connection to the submarine case. Every day, several hundred new articles tumble into our news-monitoring platforms. There are newspapers, radio stations, and television channels from places we can hardly locate on the map. *Submarine*, *Copenhagen*, and *Kim Wall* are words that orbit the world at high speed, around and around.

We're endlessly grateful for our strategy to not give any interviews, statements, or comments. If we had relaxed that rule even once, we wouldn't have gotten through this. It takes many hours per day to say no, in a friendly but firm manner, to all the inquiries that come in by telephone, email, and through other means. We know that journalists have pressure to deliver, and preferably information that nobody else has found. However, we're not the ones who will be able to help them with this task.

More than one hundred journalists from sixteen countries have been given credentials to enter the courthouse in Copenhagen. We know that Jocke and I will be the main focus of the reporters this first day in court. Everyone wants to see us, see our reactions, get to witness our first meeting with Peter Madsen. We will be sitting a few yards from him—this man who has caused us immense pain, who has ruined our lives. If Kim hadn't gone out on the submarine with him, she'd still be alive. He claims he's a captain, but a true seaman would never have gone out on the ocean alone in a fifty-nine-foot-long vessel, never mind dive to the bottom of the sea in it. The boat requires a three-person crew. There are no navigational lights on it, and there's no equipment for surfacing if there's a failure on board. Madsen ignored all of this on that Thursday in August, in the same way that he had apparently done many times before. He might never have another opportunity to demonstrate it, but he's done enough damage already to make obvious his complete lack of respect for other human beings.

One comfort during these difficult days has been our work with Kim's fund.

We're participating in the process that will help us determine which young female journalist will receive the first grant in a couple of weeks—on Kim's birthday, March 23. We have whittled the 140 applications down to 10, all of which are pitches for reporting that is important and interesting.

In order to increase interest, and in order to give the media a bone, we agree to an interview with the TT News Agency (Tidningarnas Telegrambyrå). Our conditions are the same simple ones we laid down before: We only want to talk about the fund. It's a good interview and an excellent article that is published two days before the trial. We focus on the fund and we focus on Kim's work. Maybe this can somehow balance out the incredible number of articles that focus on Madsen. We're also glad that Kim receives the Swedish Publicists' Association South's stipend posthumously for her work. We've known about it for a while, but now it's official. Once again, we emphasize Kim's career as a journalist and what she did and what she stood for. Again, the impact in the media is great. A kind of balance is created after all, even though the scale tips rather heavily to Madsen's advantage.

Thursday, March 8, 2018

The alarm clock rings early on this snowy Thursday in March, a day we've been dreading for a long time. Nonetheless, it's a day we know we have to get through somehow. It's International Women's Day, a day celebrated all over the world with demonstrations and public displays for women's equal worth and rights. We will be spending the day in room 60 in the municipal courthouse in Copenhagen.

The topic is the evening when a man and woman went out on the ocean together in a homemade submarine. Only the man came back; the woman was found later, maimed and in pieces. Now we will—maybe—get answers to all the questions that have tortured us since that August night.

During the months that have elapsed since Kim disappeared, Peter Madsen hasn't had more than a peripheral place in my life. I have followed all the events in great detail and have come to the conclusion that no matter how often I thought we had reached bottom, we always fell even further. Peter Madsen is simply a shadow figure, a person I know exists, but about whom I waste no time thinking.

It's probably a kind of defense mechanism. What energy I have, my body and I choose not to spend on him. He's not uninteresting—after all, he's been charged with robbing me of my daughter—but he's not going to be allowed to move into my soul, my mind. I have no use for hate or revenge. Even under normal circumstances, these aren't things that are typical for me, but no matter how I try, I can't feel anything but apathy toward the man who somehow caused Kim's death.

Peter Madsen has already cost us way too much, far more than any human should have to pay. If I allow myself to be caught up in feelings of hate and revenge, I'm the only one who has something to lose. He couldn't care less. Life has to win, not death. Evil can't be allowed to triumph, and now the day has come when we'll meet Peter Madsen face-to-face.

Early on we decided we would participate in the trial, at least on the first day. The reason is simple—perhaps even primitive: We want to look our daughter's murderer in the eye, and we want him to see us.

The media presence is the largest in Denmark's history. Early in the morning, the square outside the municipal courthouse—on Nytorvet, right next to the famous pedestrian street Strøget—is already full of reporters, cameras, and microphones. We don't have to run the gauntlet, fortunately. Our safe haven in the chaotic tumult is, as it's been so many times before, Jens Møller Jensen. We park next to the police station and have time for a cup of coffee before we're brought to downtown Copenhagen in an unmarked vehicle. We're able to slip into a side entrance of the large courthouse without anyone noticing us.

After going through security, we're led through narrow corridors, spiraling stairways, and the law archives, until we finally reach room 60. It's a room that reminds us more of a ballroom than the home of Lady Justice. Two majestic crystal candelabras hang from the vaulted ceiling, the windows facing the courtyard are high, and behind the dock there's a sculpture on the wall that seems a bit out of place for a courtroom. To me it seems like a person in despair, holding his head in his hands. Perhaps it's not so wrong after all—it may be that many feel that way when they enter the room. Farther back in the courtroom, there are around fifty seats, for the most part behind a barrier.

Journalists are already in their places—there was tough competition for the spots that were distributed through a special system: this many for the Danish media, this many for the Swedish, then the remainder to foreign newspapers and media companies. Another hundred or so journalists crowd into the court's cafeteria, where they will follow the proceedings on large screens.

Beside the representatives for the press, there are eight black chairs. On the seats there are laminated cards with the text "Reserved for Next of Kin." This is where we'll sit. At the very back of the room, behind the journalists, there are corresponding seats for the next of kin of the defendant.

We wait in an adjoining room. There's a thermos of coffee on the table, but it remains untouched. The time is almost nine thirty, and we decide to walk out into the large room. Jocke takes his place at the front, closest to the wall, and I sit next to him. There are one or two familiar faces among the journalists, but nobody greets anyone. Today is different: Today we're not old colleagues anymore. Today we're parents of a journalist who lost her life in the sea two hundred days ago.

I miss the moment when Peter Madsen enters the room. All of a sudden I see a person with black-framed glasses sitting at the side of his defense attorney. Although I've seen pictures of him thousands of times, I'm not entirely sure that it's Madsen. I whisper to Jocke, who's just as unsure as I am. The hair color isn't the same as in pictures and on videos, and the glasses with their distinctly thick frames are misleading.

It takes a few seconds before we're completely sure—this is the accused, the man who threw our lives into an entirely new and terrible direction last August. I meet his gaze. He understands who I am and who Jocke is. I wonder what's going through his head just now. Does he feel any remorse? Does he have any idea what kind of feelings we have? He looks down.

Then the judge comes in, and everyone stands up out of respect for her and her office. She's the one, together with two laypersons, who will determine whether Peter Madsen is guilty of the crimes he's been charged with. After the twelve days of the trial, the trio will come to a decision: acquittal or conviction. The prosecutor, Jakob Buch-Jepsen, spends a large part of the morning describing what has happened since August 10: the search for the submarine, Madsen's rescue from the sea after sinking the *Nautilus*, the search for Kim, and the finding of her body parts one after another. We've seen the pictures and videos shown on the large screens before, but it still hurts to see a smiling Kim in the submarine tower as the vessel glides out of the harbor in Copenhagen. Some of the pictures from the police's preliminary investigation are macabre; the very worst ones are reserved for the judge and laypersons only—neither we nor the journalists are allowed to see them. When pictures of body parts and the tools the prosecution believes were used to maim her body are shown, we feel the reporters' eyes on us. In Denmark, as in Sweden, photography in the courtroom is forbidden, but drawing is permissible. In the front rows, several artists are sitting, filling page after page of their drawing pads.

Madsen mostly looks down at the computer screen in front of him, but now and then he raises his eyes and looks in our direction. There's about twelve yards between his chair and our seats. After lunch he comes quite close—there might be only three yards between his place on the witness stand and our chairs. When he passes us on his way to be examined, I'm struck by how short he is. To me, Madsen seems small and stocky, slightly hunched, wearing a black T-shirt and a pair of royal-blue sweatpants that are way too big for him. He's wearing a pair of tennis shoes that swing back and forth in a nervous way during most of the examination. He often puts his hands under his thighs. Is it so nobody will see how they're shaking, or is this a habit of his?

For several hours, Peter Madsen is allowed to explain what happened on board the submarine, before and after. Since we're sitting diagonally behind him, neither we nor the reporters can see his facial expressions. He answers most of the questions cooperatively but tries to avoid others. It takes a while before the prosecutor gets to the question that's the central one for us: How did Kim die? The answer sounds well-rehearsed, but obviously Madsen has had many long hours alone in his jail cell to prepare himself. Out of consideration for us, at first he doesn't want to say what happened. Madsen thinks that it would be better for the family to believe that Kim died because the submarine hatch hit her on the head—that her death had been immediate.

Madsen says he didn't want the world to know that Kim had actually died because of a technical failure of the submarine's equipment, a flaw that allowed exhaust fumes to leak into the interior, where Kim was. Madsen himself was on the deck, and as the good sailor he was, he had of course closed the manhole so that sudden waves—on the calm sea—wouldn't be able to run down into the submarine. Hundreds of questions hang in the air of the large courtroom, where oxygen is starting to get short this afternoon. Why didn't Madsen call for help? is one of the most significant ones. He says he wasn't able to carry Kim's body up, although he tried for half an hour. Kim weighed about 110 pounds; Madsen weighed significantly more, if not double that.

We don't get any answers today. The unanswered questions are like a cliffhanger in a television series—the sequel won't be aired for thirteen days. Is the long break a coincidence, because of the availability of rooms in the municipal courthouse? Or is it a marker in a psychological game? Is the first day supposed to "sink in" before the trial continues? We don't know. When we leave the courtroom, we see that the only way out is right past Peter Madsen. There's only about eighteen inches between us as we walk by. He meets my gaze, but this time he doesn't lower his eyes. Maybe he believes that we've accepted his version of what happened.

Once again we leave the court building by a back door.

As we walk toward the unmarked police car, we can see the media circus on the square in front of the main entrance. The prosecutor has been caught by the entire corps, and we're thankful to have avoided being part of the strange performance.

There's a silver lining on this dreadful day: The fund has reached its goal of $200,000. The fact that it happened on International Women's Day feels like the work of a higher power. Whether we've heard the truth or lies in room 60 on this Thursday, Kim will continue to live. Despite everything.

CHAPTER 42

Kim spent the early summer in New York meeting editors, friends, and colleagues. Her goal, however, was to get to Copenhagen as quickly as possible. She finally crosses the Atlantic in mid-July, and she splits her time between Ole and us—mostly the former. Kim spends one weekend in Arild with Eva, a friend since her years in London, and photographs from that weekend show a young woman quite satisfied with her life. The next few years are planned out, and in a few weeks she's going to move to China with Ole.

On Tuesday, August 8, Kim is at home with us at Gislöv Beach. We pick gooseberries and red currants. We sit together at the table on the wooden deck, cleaning gooseberries and talking about this and that. Kim tells us about a visit she and Ole recently made to the home of some acquaintances on the island of Fyn, and about a wedding they're going to the following Saturday. We work a bit more on our itinerary for our China trip, which is coming up in about a month. A few hours later, we've turned the berries into marmalade. Kim writes neat labels that we glue onto the jars.

Afterward, she's in a rush to get to Malmö to see some good friends and our family's "bonus grandmother," Ann Marie.

There are so many of us who want time with Kim when she's finally on our latitude.

CHAPTER 43

It's time to award the first grantee. In-depth interviews complement the applications of the ten finalists, and through a phone meeting with jury members in Asia, the US, Helsingborg, and Gislöv Beach, we're going to elect the first recipient of the Kim Wall Grant. All along, this work with Kim's fund has been a lifeline for us. Or maybe more of a shield. Working with the fund has protected us from the reality around us, the reality that we can't really take in, or don't want to. Seeing the fund grow day by day is a comfort, a warming thought, something positive that helps us dare to look forward. There was a word that stood out for us on the computer screen the first time we read through the ten very qualified applications: *Greenland.*

All her life, Kim was fascinated by the large island. She was three years old when I went to Greenland. I came home with stories of icebergs, glaciers, and an apartheid-like policy against the Inuit. Kim, with her strong sense of justice, immediately took the side of the aboriginal residents against Denmark, the colonial power.

She had planned to go there in the spring of 2018 with Ole.

After reading through a number of applications, it was obvious to us—this was a Kim story. The parallels with her stories from the Marshall Islands are clear—the small person's fight against the system bears the clear stamp of a story Kim would have loved to have told the world. The others in the selection jury shared our opinion. Of the ten strong applications, Anne Kirstine Hermann's was the one that distinguished itself. She cries with joy when the IWMF representative calls her up. She didn't know Kim personally, but she shares her values and journalistic ideas. We call to congratulate her a few hours later, and since Anne is Danish and lives in Copenhagen, she immediately accepts our invitation to come for a visit two days later. We would really like to meet her before the ceremony in New York, and we also want her to see where Kim grew up.

Jocke and I stand on the platform at the Central Station in Trelleborg when the purple regional train rolls in. We recognize Anne right away from her profile picture on Facebook. There are big hugs and an immediate feeling of knowing each other. We converse easily—we have a lot in common and share views on several of the world's large and small problems. We enjoy each other's company, and we know that she'll become part of our big, colorful family.

Members of this worldwide constellation greet us when we land in New York the next day. We have mixed feelings traveling to the city we learned to love in large part by experiencing it through Kim's eyes.

The most important task we have is to present the first Kim Wall Grant on her birthday, March 23, but we have some difficult tasks to deal with as well. In my purse, I'm carrying the original death certificate for our daughter. It's an official document with red ribbon, seal, and stamps. We've been permitted to borrow this piece of paper from the police; it has to be returned until the case has been fully ground in the legal mills. We need the document in order to close her bank accounts as well as her accounts for gas, electricity, and internet for her apartment in Brooklyn. It's difficult to go to the bank and explain our issue. Our friend Carol is there to support us and lead us through the American system. About a half hour later, the paper shuffling is finished, and we have a check in our hands. The other matters are also rather simple to take care of with the help of the death certificate. It all feels so absurd and unreal, though. We walk down Park Avenue with a piece of paper in a plastic folder in my purse that proves that our daughter is dead—murdered and cut into pieces.

We have intense days in New York. We meet Kim's friends for lunch or dinner; we meet contacts for organizations that will help us in different ways. We visit Kim's favorite restaurants and the places we know she would have liked.

One special experience is a Chinese dim sum restaurant in Flushing. Kim was here several times, and, of course, loved it for its unusual décor: a life-sized horse. Chinese women push their carts around past our table again and again in the gigantic eatery and try to get us to buy even more dishes to fill our tables and stomachs with.

Two of Kim's schoolmates from London work at the UN now, which among other things means that we get a guided tour through the building that houses the organization that, hopefully, will serve as a guarantee that there will be world peace. Since the General Assembly isn't meeting, we get to become better acquainted with the world-famous room and even have the opportunity to try out the lectern—the same one at which many world leaders have stood. For an hour or so, our darker thoughts are chased away and we can be happy about standing in the center of world events—even though the main players aren't present. We also have a chance to see the offices of the general secretary and admire the view from the thirty-ninth floor. Kim was an intern at the UN several times, and even though she could be critical of the system—particularly after peeking behind the curtain in earthquake-ravaged Haiti—she knew that the world would be an even more dangerous place without the UN.

During the nights and early morning hours, we follow the trial's progress in Copenhagen. Live blogs and innumerable online articles provide
the smallest bit of news.

We try to shift our focus, when we can, on doing interviews for
Swedish media about the fund. Before we left Sweden, Sweden's Radio
had done a taped interview, and very late at night, at 1:30 a.m., I participate in *Morgonstudion* for SVT News via Skype. After a rather awkward
beginning, the conversation starts to flow, and once again we have the
chance to present our message about the fund, working conditions for
women journalists in general, and for freelancing women in particular.
I also emphasize Kim's work method, a model that feels rather old-
fashioned and time intensive to many. Kim was never in a hurry—she
wanted to take in the whole human, the whole situation.

Finally, Friday, March 23, arrives, the day Kim would have turned
thirty-one. In many ways, it's a heavy day, but we've decided we're going
to celebrate her birthday. It's not a sorrowful event, but rather a party,
just as it should be on a birthday. Carol surprises us this morning with
identical gifts for us and Tom: a lamp in the shape of Kim's signature gesture, the peace sign. The fingers glow in white neon. We're all
moved—such a lovely gesture that means so much. The lamp now has
a place of honor here at home, because it's Kim's lamp.

Today we've booked a very important lunch meeting with a woman
we've never met before. Even so, we share so much. Diane Foley is the
mother of James Foley, an American journalist who was kidnapped in
2012 during an assignment in Syria. James, or Jim as he was called, was
murdered by ISIS in 2014. His mother has done the same thing we're
doing: survived by focusing on drawing something positive out of the
catastrophe. Just as we've done, the family started a fund. Its orientation
is a bit different; they are working to get kidnapped Americans home
from war zones. At the same time, they want to protect independent
war correspondents so that they can continue their important work
reporting from war theaters in a more secure way. Their third goal is

to educate the public and students about the threats to democracy and freedom that the kidnapping of journalists presents.

"We believe that it's our duty to protect American citizens no matter where they are in the world," Diane Foley says. "Freedom of the press is a cornerstone of our democracy. News from conflict areas comes to an ever larger extent from independent war correspondents."

Diane Foley is a strong woman who has made her son's tragic death her reason for living. In different ways, she works to spread her message: Jim shall not have died in vain. One way is to show a film about Jim at universities all over the US. We connect over salad and hamburgers. We have so much in common, although we come from very different worlds. We're united in grief over having lost a child in a most horrific way, and in finding meaning by helping their name and memory live on.

Kim and Jim—somehow it feels like they belong together. If they had met, they would have certainly had a lot to talk about.

New York during rush hour on a Friday afternoon means traffic jams, endless red lights, and long lines. Even though we left Brooklyn in plenty of time for the presentation of Kim's grant, we're late getting there. We've promised to give a few short interviews about the fund for Danish, Swedish, Norwegian, and international media. It is stressful and a bit confusing, with interviews in English, Danish, and Swedish. As we usually do, Jocke and I help fill in each other's gaps. We know what we want to say and what we won't talk about. An attempt to get us to describe our feelings before the trial is met with a head shake, and the journalist respects that. They get the message. We talk about the worry we could never banish during all the years Kim was trotting around the globe—a worry that, however, wasn't present on that terrible Thursday night in August, because she was in Copenhagen, far away from the world's hot spots.

Tom has taken on the job of being the family's spokesperson tonight. We're happy for him to do it, because he does it so well. He speaks the best English, and he doesn't get as choked up when talking about Kim as I do. He compares Kim to a star—a star shining in the blackest darkness. He thanks everyone who's contributed to make this evening possible, and he introduces Anne, whose identity has been a complete secret up until now.

Spontaneous applause bursts forth. Anne feels so right, and her speech goes straight to our hearts.

> *I accept this award with mixed feelings today. On the one hand, I'm so honored to be able to participate in this celebration of Kim's life and work. With great humility I receive this trust to continue her journalistic legacy further. I'm happy that this grant will give me the opportunity to do this work—to wear out shoe leather, something lacking in media to a great extent now. On the other hand, this memorial grant aims a searchlight on a few painful truths. Men and women are still not equal. Men and women are not equally safe. This is true in Scandinavia as well, where Kim and I grew up. Hate against women has no ethnicity, no nationality, no religion. Women reporters are in the risk zone not only in areas suffering under armed conflicts.*

> *Reporting, particularly in the feature genre, is a way of working in which you often find yourself alone with strangers you are going to interview. We ride in cars with some, visit others in their homes. How can you see the world through their eyes if you don't? Having access to this is one of the requirements, nothing one can choose or not choose. No safety measures can protect us from unjustified, meaningless violence.*

It is our collective responsibility to discourage and prevent this, not the individual journalist's job.

A good journalist's responsibility, as I see it, is to stimulate curiosity and empathy between people. It is an important democratic task that Kim mastered in an impressive way by looking for what she called rebellious undertones. This is a task that seems to be even more important in these times in which quality journalism is under pressure from many directions and, hence, so is democracy.

Even though I didn't know Kim, I share her ideals and interests. She liked combining her on-the-ground-shoe-leather reporting with the approach of a foreign correspondent. The project that the grant will help me to conduct is in many ways reminiscent of Kim's stories, particularly those she made from the Marshall Islands. Just like Kim, I'll be traveling to faraway communities in order to report on how they have been affected by colonialism and the Cold War, stories that have been ignored for decades. In Greenland, I will interview people who were driven away from their land because the Danish authorities wanted to concentrate the population and assimilate it to Danish culture. I will interview people who were taken from their parents when they were children and raised as ideal Danes.

These are patterns we recognize from colonial times, but they've brought me to a larger story, a story that reports on how these innocent children became a part of Denmark's plan to gain control over Greenlandic territory, although colonialism was prohibited after the UN was established.

This is the story of a secret colony.

I'm not trying to fool myself into believing that my report-ing is comparable to Kim's or can replace it. But striving to achieve her level gives me enormous motivation. Unlike Kim, I haven't yet had my work published in American media, and I'm very thankful for the possibility of working with one of her editors to get my reporting to a larger public.

I want to express my admiration for the dedication that Kim's family and friends have shown during the last horrific months by starting a fund in her name. I also want to show my deep-est gratitude for the interest in my project and that you chose me for this first grant. Thank you for your trust and for your encouragement, which means that I can execute this project in my own way.

Finally: Thanks, Kim, that you are a journalistic beacon for generations of women to come.

Kim isn't gone—she's with us, and her name is being spread all over the world. Her work will be spoken about for many years to come. In his speech, Tom mentions that if he's done the math correctly, the fund should be able to distribute grants for at least forty years. "I'll be an old man then," he realizes, very aware of the fact that for the rest of his life, he will have the task of continuing his murdered sister's life and work.

The evening is topped off with an unusual performance. It's a Haitian Vodou artist playing her own music. She's asked if she can perform in Kim's honor. The musician and Kim met when our daugh-ter was working on a story about Vodou, and they became friends. Val Jeanty talks about light and about Kim, saying "*Ayi bobo* Kim—Kim is the light."

On Saturday, hundreds of thousands of people march all over the United States to protest gun laws and school shootings. Kim would have been one of the marchers—carrying the double-sided sign that says "Not One More" on one side and "Never Again" on the other. I find such a poster on the street late in the afternoon—it's a little worn and has a shoe print on it. For us the messages are frighteningly relevant and go right into our bodies: not one more—never again. Let this be true for all people—schoolchildren in the US and journalists all over the world.

CHAPTER 44

We land in Copenhagen late Monday afternoon. The next morning we'll be back in the Danish capital for a new day of the trial.

On Tuesday, Iso looks at us. We've just come home to him and our beloved beach—why are we leaving again? Kim's cousin Marie will take care of him today, taking him on long walks, petting him, giving him closeness and receiving it in return. In some strange way, being together with Iso is very comforting. His unconditional love and devotion warm us and give us strength. He demands so little and gives so much.

That morning as we drive over the Öresund Bridge, we realize we've lost count of how many times we've made this trip since last August. We look out over the railing—on both sides of this connector between Sweden and Denmark, Peter Madsen sailed with our daughter, Kim, on that night in August. Where exactly did she die? Part of me wants to know, the other part doesn't. It's enough to know that somewhere out on this peaceful sea, on this narrow strait between two countries, our daughter's life was taken.

The days of the trial bring long lines of witnesses who contribute different pieces of the puzzle; somehow these pieces are supposed to give the judge and her two jury members an understanding of what happened so that they can make their decision. One of these days, we act as witnesses—not for the case itself, but for the decision on damages. We tell about our relationship to Kim, how we stayed in contact, and about the time after the catastrophe. We tell about the 69,000 newspaper articles that were written, about the feeling of having shrunk from professional journalists into just parents, the parents everyone knows, at least in our hometown. We talk about the loss of our private lives, about Kim's relationship with Ole. Everything is filtered through an interpreter who is there to translate our Swedish into Danish. The hearings are quickly taken care of, and it's such a relief to go back to the chairs reserved for family. I'm doubtful that the defendant has listened—he seems preoccupied with something else. He often looks in our direction, and he seems to be very aware that we're present in the room. He's asked that we be told not to pass him when we walk out of or into the courtroom—he's upset by this. We are forced to respect his opinion and take the longer way by the judge's bench instead.

The prosecutor, Jakob Buch-Jepsen, warns us: "This afternoon we'll show videos that were found on the defendant's computer." Some of the videos—the worst ones—will only be shown to the legal team, while others are shown on the large screen for all present. The ones we get to see are animated and represent decapitations and other forms of violent death through unthinkable brutality.

We feel the reporters' eyes on us and try to look as neutral as possible. How can there be a market for something so horrific? Who draws stories like this, and what are those people like who watch such videos? The other videos, the ones that only the court has to view, are accompanied by sounds that reach every corner of the courtroom. Not much of an imagination is required to figure out what images accompany such dreadful screams.

On the last day of the trial, deliberations take place in another courtroom. The final arguments and sentencing will come later. We end up in seats far back in the room, and at times it's hard to hear.

However, the advantage is that the reporters have to turn around to see our reactions to what is said by the prosecutor and defense attorney. Some of the things the prosecutor reads from the forensic psychiatric report hurt us badly:

"I don't want any corpses on my submarine."

"What do you do if you have a big problem? You divide it up into smaller ones, of course."

The prosecutor's voice is calm and factual as he reads from the text. It takes a little while before the words sink in. Or maybe they don't—this is, after all, about Kim.

A few weeks pass before it's time for the final arguments. The previous times we've driven over the Öresund Bridge, there's been snow and rain. Today the sun is shining, and we can feel spring in the air.

Even so, we have the same feeling of discomfort as we drive past the area in Öresund where Kim lost her life. We now know rather precisely where it happened: near an old military fort. We know approximately when, but we don't know how. We'll probably never find out. There's only one person who knows, and he doesn't want to say anything. Or maybe he's lying—he's done that so many times before.

The prosecutor refers to this lack of credibility in Madsen as one of the points in his closing argument. Jakob Buch-Jepsen weaves a cloth of evidence and proof to try to convict the defendant and give him a life sentence in prison. After lunch, the defense attorney has her say. She constructs a chain of events, but the difference is that Madsen is only guilty of cutting up Kim's body and dumping it in the ocean. According to the attorney, Madsen should be released since he would have only had a six-month sentence for what he's done. Life in prison or freedom: in less than forty-eight hours, we'll know the answer.

Peter Madsen gets the last word. He looks toward the seats where our family sits, where we are in the first row. A short sentence leaves his lips: "I'm very sorry."

What's he sorry about? Does he feel sorry for himself, because the submarine will be confiscated? Because his wife has left him? Because his workshop will be emptied and rented to another person? We won't know, and we don't get to hear one word about forgiveness.

Whether you choose to listen to the prosecutor's version or the defense attorney's version of what happened on that moonlit August night, Kim died then and there. She'll never come back to us, to Ole, to her friends, to her pens, her notebooks and computer, her interview subjects, her stories.

We have mixed feelings as we drive back over the bridge. We're relieved that the long trial days are now over, but we're also worried about what the decision will be. Will Madsen go free? Will he be able to walk out of the courtroom a free man? At 1:00 p.m. on Wednesday, April 25, the judge will determine his guilt and sentence him. I still don't feel hate toward this man. I don't feel anything. I'm thankful I can react this way. For me, to do otherwise would be fatal. I need my strength to go on, to make a stand for Kim and her ideals.

On Tuesday, we're on our way to the US once again—the third time in six months. Last October we had agreed to perform an honorary duty for the OPC, the Overseas Press Club of America. We'll light a candle in memory of all the journalists who have died, been injured, or been kidnapped while performing their work.

Last October, neither we nor anyone else knew that the sentence would be announced a few hours after we land in New York. Coincidence perhaps, but for us it meant we could avoid the media circus with its epicenter, Nytorvet Square, in front of the municipal courthouse in Copenhagen. At Kastrup, something happens that will mean so much to us. The line through security is long, as usual; so many people and so many belongings have to go through the machines. A gray-haired woman about my age suddenly leaves her post behind the belt at the X-ray machine and comes up to us. "May I give you a hug? I recognize you from TV. All of Denmark is behind you. May the verdict go your way." Her hug is warm and tender, and this entirely unexpected expression of sympathy affects us deeply. So kind, so warm—so human.

We don't get much sleep that first night in New York. When it's 1:00 p.m. in Copenhagen, it's 7:00 a.m. in New York, and the combination of jet lag and anxiety over missing the sentencing makes us toss and turn in bed, constantly checking the clock.

Long before 7:00 a.m., we're connected by computer, phone, and tablet. We know the verdict and sentencing will be broadcast by television with a few minutes' delay. This means that the newspapers will be the first to get the news published on the internet. The first one to do so is *Aftonbladet*, thereafter all the others—the Swedish and Danish newspapers, the *New York Times*, and CNN.

Peter Madsen is sentenced to the harshest punishment possible according to Danish law: life in prison.

Our feelings are once again ambivalent. Justice has been served and Kim has been vindicated, but so what? She won't come back to us, no matter what punishment is meted out to that man. In addition, we're quickly told that we'll be going through the same hell again, because Madsen is filing an appeal with the Eastern High Court. This isn't the end; we've just made it down one part of the road. The next few months will continue to offer anxiety, desperation, and hope.

The OPC dinner is an amazing event that brings together the best of American foreign correspondents. Around twenty prizes in different categories will be presented to these journalists who work all over the globe. We've been seated at the table of honor together with the keynote speaker and the master of ceremonies. Many are moved by Kim's fate, both those who knew her personally and those who've followed the story since August. Kim has become a concern for the reporting corps in a large part of the world. Everyone says, "We would have done the same thing—we would have gone out in the submarine, too. We can't let this silence us; we can't be afraid."

When we walk onto the stage before the six hundred guests dressed in tuxedos and ball gowns, we have a sense of unrealness. Jocke lights the candle, and I speak:

> *We wish we didn't have to stand here today. We wish we had been sitting at that table out there as proud parents, getting to see our daughter, Kim, accept a prize for one of her assignments. We wish that no journalists anywhere in the world would need to die or be injured while they're doing their important work. We hope that there won't be a need to light any memorial candles in the years to come.*

An hour or so later, we once again go up onstage, this time to present the first Kim Wall Best Digital Reporting Award. It goes to the *Washington Post* for a multimedia report on the Palestinians and their quality of life. This is a story that Kim might have done, that she would have wanted to do. This important story is now honored with a prize in Kim's name.

CHAPTER 45

Wednesday, August 9, 2017

We're going to try to pull together our annual family photography session. The only possibility is a Wednesday morning. Ever since Kim was a bit more than one year old and Tom was still in utero, we've taken a picture of our family. We often take it at the same time of year, and always in the same spot in the garden. The pictures have been hung on the wall, one after the other, in the hall outside Kim's room. With the years, our collection has grown, and although we pass the pictures many times a day, we often stop to look at them and remember. Maybe it's a sweater that catches our eye, or how the children have grown, the dogs, the student cap, or some other detail. Our picture wall is usually noticed by our guests, and, for us, it's terribly important. This is the history of our family—thirty years of the Wall family distilled down to a few square yards.

In recent years, it's been more difficult to get the picture taken because Kim has often been in another part of the world. But we've always made it work, and now we're going to see to it that Picture No. 30 is also taken. We need to do some fiddling with our schedules. Tom's working the evening shift and isn't happy about getting up early. Kim needs to pick up Ole at the station in Hyllie after our photo shoot.

With a little give-and-take in all directions, the family finally assembles early in the morning. Sometimes it takes a while for the logistics to be worked out, everyone finding their spots in the opening in the fence on the south side of our yard, the dog strategically placed in the center. But with thirty years' experience, the whole thing goes quickly and smoothly. Iso cooperates, the sun is in the correct position so nobody is squinting, and the timer works. We take the picture and realize that it's number thirty and that the lowest row is now complete. However, there's room for at least one more row. After that, we'll have to figure out something else. Nobody would even imagine that there wouldn't be a Picture No. 31. The family tradition is strong, and it's intended to continue for many, many years to come. Maybe a quick thought about a third generation has flown by, that there might be more people in the picture.

After the photo session, we sit together in the kitchen, chatting. The siblings haven't seen each other for a while, and Kim compliments Tom on his new sneakers. Then Tom leaves for another workday at *Helsingborgs Dagblad*. Kim borrows my car to drive to Hyllie, outside Malmö, to pick up Ole at the train. As mothers do, I ask her if she knows where she's going after she picks him up, and I point out that the map in my car is probably as old as the car—that is, twenty years old. Kim answers with a big smile on her face: "Together we have three and a half, maybe four, master's degrees. I think we can get to Kullen and back."

I can't think of a good answer to this, of course, and wish them a lovely day. Kim and Ole are planning to drive to Kullaberg on the Kullen Peninsula and have a closer look at Lars Vilks's driftwood sculpture *Nimis*. In the evening they'll be back in Trelleborg, and we're going to eat dinner together. We're going to get to meet Ole for the first time—the man in Kim's life for a year now. Finally, Kim thinks the time is right, and we're looking forward to meeting him. We've heard so much about him and have had the chance to form an impression about this man Kim wants to spend her life with. Now we'll get to see if our impression is correct.

During the day, we get pictures by cell phone from their climb at Kullaberg and a picture of a sandwich cake, a savory cake layered like a sandwich. This may seem to be a strange thing to take on a picnic, but there's an explanation. Ole has never eaten sandwich cake; this delicacy doesn't exist in Denmark, land of that divine dish smørrebrød. It's late before Kim and Ole are back in Trelleborg, but finally my old red Volvo pulls in. Out hop Kim and Ole. There he is—Kim's partner. Soon we're sitting at our table in the restaurant Bistrå, which is tucked into an old grain warehouse in the harbor. The walls are decorated with old pictures from the previous turn of the century, and it feels more like someone's living room than a restaurant. Kim and Ole have much to tell about their car trip and visit to Kullaberg. We connect with Ole immediately, and the conversation flows as if we've known each other a long time. And in a way, we have.

We also share our love for Kim, who this evening is glowing from a newly acquired sunburn thanks to an entire day out in nature—and her feelings for Ole. We talk about this and that—about computer games Ole designs, among other things, about the upcoming trip to China, about our visit and the side trips we'll take together. Kim and Ole say that they'll be going to Greenland in the spring, and then, of course, we get into the trip I made there many years ago. Suddenly, it's very late, and we're the last guests left in the restaurant. Before I drive Kim and Ole to the train that will take them back to Copenhagen, we have time to look at the gigantic mural on the wall in Ångkvarnen, painted by Johan Falkman. It's a depiction of the development of Trelleborg's harbor over the past one hundred years, and it's over seven hundred square feet in size. Kim can proudly claim that her grandfather—my father—can be found in two places on the mural.

We wave goodbye to Kim and Ole outside the Central Station and wish them a safe trip back to Refshale Island. Jocke and I sit for a while after we get home, and we agree that Ole is just as pleasant as we had expected and hoped. We're happy, and thankful that Kim's found someone she wants to spend her life with. We're happy to know that now she won't be alone in China if something were to happen. They're a couple, and they can help each other and take care of each other. That evening we go to bed feeling good in body and soul.

CHAPTER 46

In all the days we spend at the municipal court in Copenhagen, there's something missing. For hours and hours, we've heard about stab wounds, hard disks, vents, text messages, and sharpened screwdrivers. We've heard descriptions of blood stains on clothes, straps, bags with their contents, water hoses, and Madsen's previously published blog pieces on heaven and hell.

But where's Kim? Nowhere. She's almost never mentioned by name—it's as if she doesn't exist, although it's all about her. Our beautiful, ambitious daughter, full of joie de vivre, isn't there in the courtroom. Her picture should be shown on the large screen the whole time. Her smile should pain every single person sitting there. Why isn't she present? Why is she being reduced to something vague that's named in a dependent clause? The focus is entirely on the man who's been charged with having caused her death—Kim herself is forgotten.

She does come to life briefly when Ole talks about her. About how Kim saw beauty in everything, about her curiosity, her drive, her strong will. And she appears before us as a living, breathing human for a few minutes as we describe our relationship to our daughter.

She flashes by us when the prosecutor mentions something found in Kim's jacket pocket: a train ticket between Kastrup and Trelleborg. Then she disappears again, into the fog behind all the technicalities.

We get to hear about crushed dreams and plans, but it isn't Kim's wishes and future that are being discussed. Nobody is talking about the loss our family has sustained, as have so many friends all over the world. Nobody seems to care about all the articles that will remain unwritten, about the people whose voices will remain unheard. Nobody is talking about the person, Kim, the journalist who was simply doing her job, who never returned from what was supposed to be a routine assignment. Nobody tells about the plans and hopes she and Ole had for their life together.

The prosecutor makes an attempt and points to a portrait of Kim in Compendium 3 of 23 that contain all the parts of the investigation. One single page of perhaps five thousand is devoted to Kim, the human being.

CHAPTER 47

On a windy day in April, we have an appointment with the funeral director. We've postponed this visit. We don't really want to have to take care of this task. We've visited this place on similar occasions when parents who've passed away were to be buried. That was natural, clearly in order, but this isn't.

The room is large and bright, with white walls and an oval wood table. On it are two small red glass candleholders, a bowl of candies sporting the company logo, and a small package of tissues—these, too, imprinted on the packaging with the logo. We talk about the time and place, practical things that must be attended to. We haven't prepared ourselves, and we go by gut feelings—what kind of funeral would Kim have wanted? The thought makes me dizzy. No thirty-year-old thinks about her funeral, but we try to make decisions anyway. In some inexplicable way, we feel rather good once the date is pinned down, the place determined, and we can let our family know. This is one more step along the road that we wish no parent would ever have to walk.

The same evening, we're met by yet another wave of empathy. We're standing on the stage at the restaurant Inkonst in Malmö. We're there to accept the Swedish Publicists' Association's prize that's been awarded to Kim.

Csaba Bene Perlenberg, the chair of the Publicists' Association South, talks about Kim, whom he's never met, but has gotten to know through us. He says that Kim's fate has affected many: "There are just as many people who have been deeply moved by the strength that the entire Wall family has shown these past months. You simply can't find braver and stronger people," he says, and continues. "The stipend goes to Kim Wall, but we're very proud to be able to turn it over to Ingrid and Joachim."

In explaining the award, he mentions that "Kim is a world-class journalist with a unique ability to find and write the stories and human fates that mirror our globalized times."

I've prepared a short speech, but once again, my feelings overtake me. I don't know if my words, half muffled by tears, reach the audience, but I see how they all stand in sympathy. In some way, I'm able to offer thanks on behalf of Kim and the fund.

CHAPTER 48

May–June 2018

I'm in the middle of an article for the web when the phone rings. It's Sweden's Radio, but not one of the reporters for our local station asking about a municipal issue. The question comes as a surprise: Would I like to be one of the summer hosts for *Summer on P1*? I should have probably thought a bit before I answered, but I accepted the offer immediately. Such an honor! The summer program has existed almost as long as I have. It's a classic program that is just as much a part of summer in Sweden as the midsummer pole and mosquito bites. Now things go quickly—in a few days, everything is organized. I write the manuscript, talk to the producer, book my ticket to Stockholm. Everything is very secret—nothing can leak out before the press conference at Berwaldhallen in front of a massive media presence.

Then I'm standing there onstage with a crown of flowers in my hair. Around me I see many familiar faces; some are very new acquaintances.

I'm not prepared for the attention from journalists once the official part is over.

After all, I'm usually the one who's on the other side of the notebook and pen. Now I'm the one who has to answer questions. And I do just that. I see the opportunity to let Kim come forward, take her place. I make use of the chance to talk about Kim and what she wanted to do with her life. Maybe I can strip away at least part of the picture of her as a crime victim and replace it with the image of a gifted, involved professional reporter.

A week or so later, I'm sitting in the radio studio in Malmö talking about Kim—about our lives during the year that's passed, about light and darkness, about the fact that life goes on despite everything. It's a rather large studio on the third floor of the Radiohuset, headquarters of Sweden's Radio, on Baltzarsgatan in Malmö. The producer, Anna Landelius, meets Jocke and me with a big hug, coffee at the ready, and a glass of water. I'm completely safe and feel great confidence in Anna and the sound technician, Saga. The large headphones cover my ears, the microphone is adjusted and volume tested. The doors to the control room are closed, and I get a thumbs-up from Anna. All there is to do now is to begin: "The quiet of our bedroom is pierced by a ringing phone. The red numbers projected on the ceiling show 5:31 a.m.," I read.

At times, my feelings take over, and the tears form a lump in my throat. That's the way it is, and that's the way it's allowed to be. Grief and loss overtake us from time to time, sometimes when we least expect it. I don't care anymore if someone sees me, if someone thinks it's odd. We live with our grief every day, around the clock, and we're permitted to be sad.

I talk about our grief and about how we've chosen to try to see the light, even when it can't get any darker. I talk about how we want people to act around us. It's our hope that people won't try to stay away, that they won't cross the street to avoid seeing us. My advice is just as simple as it is difficult: You don't have to say anything or ask how we are. Just give me a hug—that goes a long way.

The music I choose has a connection to Kim in some way. Björn Afzelius's "Isabelle" is an obvious choice, just like Frank Sinatra's "My Way." The final tune has the same theme: "Go Your Own Way," performed by Lissie.

The recording goes well, and we're even finished before lunch. There are still a few weeks before the program will be broadcast. It will go on the air on the tenth of August, the first anniversary of Kim's death. A few days later, we're back at the studio on Baltzarsgatan. The executives for *Summer on P1* in Stockholm want me to record the program in English, too. They believe there's substantial interest in my story in the English-speaking world. This is a little more difficult. English isn't as natural, but with guidance from Anna and Saga, we record an English version, too.

I'm not really prepared for all the reactions that come in when the program is broadcast on the anniversary. The podcast version is released at 7:00 a.m., and soon the phone starts to ring and my social media accounts are full of comments. It seems as if every single person has listened to the program.

It makes me proud and happy. So do all the letters I get from people who write that they've been so moved and who thank me for being able to convey a sense of hope despite everything. Many say that they've gotten a different picture of Kim after my summer program—the picture I'm so determined to convey, the picture of a young, talented journalist who wanted to make the world a little better.

CHAPTER 49

Friday, June 1, 2018

It's a beautiful day in early summer when we say our final farewells to Kim. The sun shines in a blue sky, and the Baltic, still for once, glitters. We've chosen to have the ceremony outdoors just a few hundred yards from our home. Here Kim played as a child, jogged as a grown woman, walked the dog, enjoyed the peace so far away from the stress and bustle of some huge metropolis.

This is an end, a step along the way, but an incredibly heavy one. Once the guests have taken their seats, Jocke carries in the black urn with Kim's ashes; I follow after him with Tom and Ole. I'm carrying the portrait of Kim, which I place on a pedestal next to the urn. It is simple, beautiful, and so incredibly sad. Afterward, Jocke says, "That's the heaviest burden I've ever had to carry."

We don't call it a funeral—it's a final farewell. The message has gone out on the grapevine all over the world. We wanted absolutely no television cameras destroying this time, and there aren't any.

Although many of the guests are journalists, today they're all Kim's friends, not professionals. As comrades, they want to say goodbye and dare to show their feelings without being followed around by hungry camera lenses.

And the friends come from all over the world. The guest who travels the farthest comes from Australia. Others come from the US, Norway, Denmark, Germany, and other countries. Soon there are around one hundred of us sitting on chairs on the lawn that has already turned brown because of the lack of rain in May.

It ends up being a lovely farewell, just as we wanted. The municipal official describes Kim in a way that gets us to smile through our tears. When the last guests have placed their flowers and said their goodbyes, I suddenly see a butterfly flitting around the flowers. The beautiful creature with its delicate wings moves from one blossom to the next. For me, it's a symbol that Kim is still with us, if in an entirely different form.

We end the ceremony by walking a few hundred yards across the beach meadows to Kim's heart. We each take a stone and place it on the edge; others take our cue and do the same. The letters *K-I-M* formed by stones from the sea say everything in their simplicity. One journey is over; another one has begun.

CHAPTER 50

When we look through Kim's laptop during the fall, we find almost fourteen thousand photos that she took during her trips. We knew that she was talented with a camera as well as with a pen, but we had no idea that she had taken so many photos while traveling. The idea slowly takes shape that we could create an exhibit with some of them.

We ask Trelleborg's head of culture and leisure, Jörgen Flink, what he thinks of the idea. Does he think it would be possible to dedicate a few walls, for example at the library? He says that he could do better than that. The next day, the plan for an outdoor exhibit is born, and in April we get word from the Kockska Foundation in Trelleborg that they will provide funding.

In the middle of June, we open the exhibit, which consists of thirty-nine standing screens, each around six feet tall, put together into three-sided pillars. The screens help the viewer follow Kim's footsteps from North Korea in the east to the Marshall Islands in the west. The pictures do the talking, accompanied by brief excerpts from some of her stories.

Here you see the expressionless faces of the soldiers in North Korea's demilitarized zone, the woman in Tibet rinsing her wash in a small stream, the knife grinder in Kampala using his bicycle as a tool, the small Indian girl holding a baby bird in her hands, the skull with light bulbs in its eye sockets in Haiti, and some cool guys in Cuba.

The exhibit is kept up for almost two months on Algatan. Thousands of people pass along the pedestrian street every day. Tourists and residents of Trelleborg stop, look, and read. Many get to know Kim by doing so. She tells her stories through the pictures and takes the visitor on a trip around the world. She lets the pictures show that we are all human beings even though we live under very different conditions. She also shows that even if you were born in a midsized Swedish city, you can have the entire world as your field of work.

When we take down the exhibit at the end of the summer, we're secure in the knowledge that the image of Kim has become even more nuanced.

CHAPTER 51

Friday, August 10, 2018

As the one-year anniversary of Kim's disappearance approached, we knew only too well how it might be. The media would once again force us to experience that Thursday night in August last year. We didn't want to do that.

In the middle of April, I ate lunch with a former colleague, Lotta Wahlqvist. Sitting at the small table in the Thai restaurant in Trelleborg, Lotta asked how she could contribute to Kim's memorial fund. A former journalist herself, she wanted to do her part. I remembered the meeting with Diane Foley a few months earlier. One way to draw more money into Jim's fund was to arrange a run every year in October in New York. "Can we do the same thing here in Trelleborg?" I asked Lotta, who I know is an avid triathlete. "Of course we can!" she answered with enthusiasm. "I'm going to see Lotta Kellander tonight, and I'll see what she says."

The day after, *"Spring för Kim"* is a reality, and we decide to hold the run on the anniversary day, to honor Kim and life.

The entrance fee in its entirety will go to the fund. We imagine there will be about a hundred runners who will walk or run on this Friday evening in the beach meadows near our home and Kim's stone heart. In the US, Kim's friend since her time in Lund, Mia Dahlgren Winther, responds to the idea. She comes up with the idea of a global event called "Run for Kim."

And, in fact, a global event it becomes, with the help of a mobile app and a home page. Kim's friends get involved and arrange races in Beijing, in the Philippines, in New York, in San Francisco, and many other places. Journalists who didn't know her but who've been moved by her story arrange runs in Istanbul and Copenhagen. In all, there are fifteen places in twelve different countries that have a "Run for Kim." In addition, we hear that people have run in Kim's honor in Vanuatu, Phuket, South Africa, Ireland, and many other places.

For our original *"Spring för Kim"* at Nybostrand outside Trelleborg, six hundred people show up to either run or walk. We had to cut off sign-ups two weeks earlier. It turns out to be a fantastic evening. Together, we remember Kim and honor her. She would have enjoyed being part of the event—talking to people and creating something beautiful together. The "Run for Kim" will be an annual event, and next year we hope to get every part of the globe to join in.

In Copenhagen, Anne Kirstine Hermann, the journalist who received the first Kim Wall Grant, ran. Next year, we hope she'll have the next grant winner as company. The run didn't only provide an opportunity to get together: Money for the fund was brought in as well. In Trelleborg alone, an additional 150,000 Swedish kronor (about $16,000) was earned. In the rest of the world, Kim's friends made more than $4,000.

When we get home late that evening, we're tired. Behind us was a long day full of interviews on radio, television, and newspapers, as well as meetings with hundreds of people. We're thankful that a day that could have been so utterly dreadful ended up being the complete opposite. It was a day full of love, community, and strength. Kim has such power that even one year after her death, she can unite people across the entire globe.

Three hundred sixty-five days. Three hundred sixty-five nights. It's been a year since Kim boarded that homemade submarine in Copenhagen. Twelve months full of horror during which we've been forced to accept that Kim will never come home to us again. We can accept this, but never understand it.

We'll continue to work on keeping Kim's memory alive. Some wise person once said that as long as your name is spoken, you're still alive. Kim will continue to live and be a symbol of good journalism, curiosity, and the art of storytelling. The fund is one way to do this, "Run for Kim" is another, and a third way is the photography exhibit. The story will take other shapes, but Kim will still be the main character.

For us, Kim will always be in our thoughts. We live in our memories of her, and they will be kept alive for a long, long time.

CHAPTER 52

Thursday, August 10, 2017

It's our last day of vacation here at home, and tomorrow we're going to travel to Berlin to celebrate our wedding anniversary. On Wednesday we go back to work, so we're taking advantage of our last free days. As usual, I take Iso and walk about a mile west to Gislöv Harbor. I'm thinking about Kim as I walk, about her happy face last night, about her worries that there was still trash in my car that she hadn't remembered to pick up.

I give her a call and we talk for a long time. We talk about the good-bye party they're going to have for a few friends that evening. About the wedding she and Ole will go to on Saturday. About how we're going to Berlin the morning after. Kim asks if we're driving through Denmark on our way home, and when she finds out we are, asks us to come by Refshale Island on Tuesday evening to wish her good luck for the trip to China and to give her a high five.

I say it might be late, but Kim dismisses my reservation, saying she'll be up anyway since Ole will have left earlier that day and she'll be alone in Copenhagen for another day.

She wants to give us a hug before the long trip eastward. I promise we'll come by—a hug from Kim is worth the detour through Copenhagen. Jokingly I tell her that Ole gets high marks from us, and I advise her to hold on to him. "Don't worry—he's the one. So you'd better get used to having him around for the rest of our lives," she replies. I'm happy and a little moved when I hear my daughter say these words. She's had boyfriends, of course, but the fact that she so clearly declares her feelings and says she's found the love of her life feels like a very significant moment.

The first days after the catastrophe hit us, I thought a lot about why she didn't tell us about the planned trip on the submarine and the interview with the inventor. It would have been just like Kim to tell us about a future adventure. Or didn't she want to worry me? We soon got an answer. When we spoke on the phone, Kim hadn't yet been in touch with Peter Madsen. They had contact late in the afternoon, after the farewell party had already started. That job she had started in March looked like it would bear fruit after all. During the previous months, Kim hadn't worked as much, she complained in a message to a friend: *See what love has done to me—I can't get anything done!*

But now Kim had finally gotten in touch with the interview subject she's been looking for. She walks the few hundred yards to Madsen's hangar. Ole stays behind, starting the grill and waiting for the first guests.

About half an hour later, Kim returns and tells Ole that Madsen has agreed to be interviewed. This will happen on board his submarine that very same evening. Kim is a little hesitant, because friends have already arrived, the evening sun is shining, and she really wants to spend this last evening with her guests. At the same time, the idea of doing a quick interview is appealing—she'll be away for just a few hours and will then have a good article to sell. Her wallet needs a refill before the year in China.

Kim discusses the choice with Ole. Does he want to come with her? Should Kim stay at the party? Finally, they agree that Kim will go out on the submarine and Ole will entertain their guests. It's just a few hours, after all, and soon Kim will be back and can join the party. Ole walks with Kim partway to the submarine, which is right next to the small grassy area where the friends have gathered. A little while later, they see Kim in her bright orange sweater leaving the little harbor. She's standing in the submarine tower, with her typical hair knot on top of her head and her cell phone in her hand. She looks happy and excited—she's traveled in many kinds of vehicles, but never in a submarine.

Kim sends Ole a picture from her phone—a crab sitting on the outside of one of the submarine's windows. Soon one more picture, the conning tower, accompanied by the text *I get to steer it too!* Another text message: *I'm still alive. I love you.* Followed by eight exclamation points.

The wind turbines in the picture from the cell phone show that the submarine is on its way toward Middelgrund, an old fortress at the entrance to Copenhagen. A final message dings on Ole's phone: *He even brought coffee and cookies on board.*

Afterward, there's only silence.

TIMELINE OF EVENTS

Thursday, August 10, 2017

Around 7:00 p.m.: Kim Wall boards the homebuilt vessel *Nautilus* at Refshale Island in Copenhagen. During the following hour, the submarine is observed by several people at the entrance to Copenhagen Harbor. Kim is waving and looks happy standing in the tower of the boat.

Around 10:00 p.m.: Kim's partner, Ole, begins to worry. Kim was only supposed to be gone for a couple of hours, and it's beginning to get very dark.

Friday, August 11, 2017

2:30 a.m.: Ole alerts the police and the Coast Guard since the submarine has not returned to its dock.

3:39 a.m.: Danish police receive an alarm about a suspected accident at sea. Early in the morning, the search starts for the submarine *UC3 Nautilus*.

Helicopters and boats participate in the search.

10:30 a.m.: The submarine is located in Køge Bay. Radio contact is made with the submarine, and its "captain," Peter Madsen, reports that he is on his way back to the harbor. Everyone on board is fine according to the report.

Around 11:00 a.m.: The submarine suddenly sinks. Peter Madsen is rescued by the crew of a pleasure boat, but there is no trace of the journalist Kim Wall.

Peter Madsen is brought on land in Dragør. Madsen reports that he feels fine, but he is a bit sad that his boat has sunk.

Around 1:30 p.m.: The police announce that they will try to enter the submarine, which lies on the bottom of Køge Bay. The attempt, however, is unsuccessful because the boat is too unstable in its position on the sea floor. In the afternoon, a forensic examination is made of Peter Madsen in order to secure traces of DNA, among other things.

5:44 p.m.: The police announce that Peter Madsen is a murder suspect. He denies the crime and claims that he dropped Kim Wall off at Refshale Island on Thursday night around 10:30 p.m.

Saturday, August 12, 2017

Around 10:00 a.m.: Danish authorities begin the salvage operations of the *UC3 Nautilus*. During the morning, the preparatory hearing is held in the court in Copenhagen. The name of the journalist who has disappeared is made public.

The detention hearing is postponed, but takes place in the afternoon. Peter Madsen wants to have the hearing in open court.

The prosecutor and the judge are of a different opinion; one reason is consideration for the family. The courtroom is full of journalists and interested members of the public.

Peter Madsen is detained; however, it's not for murder as the prosecutor demands but rather for "negligence," comparable to the Swedish expression "causing the death of another."

Sunday, August 13, 2017

During the late evening, the *UC3 Nautilus* is towed to Nordhavnen, where the boat is set up behind a fence.

The work emptying the submarine of over nine thousand gallons of water is begun, as is the technical investigation.

Around 10:00 in the morning, the forensic team can enter the submarine.

11:30 a.m.: The police hold a press conference and report that no body has been found inside the submarine. The head of the investigation, Chief of Police Jens Møller Jensen, also says that there is clear evidence that the submarine was sunk intentionally. Previously, Peter Madsen had said that the boat sank after he had problems with one of the ballast tanks.

During the entire day, the search for Kim Wall continues on land, on sea, and from the air.

Monday, August 14, 2017

The search continues, and the surveillance cameras on Refshale Island are looked through, particularly in the area where Madsen claims that he dropped off the journalist.

Madsen denies having committed any crime but accepts his detention.

Wednesday, August 16, 2017

The definition of the offense is changed to "Causing the death of another under particularly aggravating circumstances." Tips continue to stream in to the police in both Denmark and Sweden.

Thursday, August 17, 2017

The police thank those who have submitted tips, and now say that they are preparing themselves to look for a dead body. The search is conducted primarily in Køge Bay.

Saturday, August 19, 2017

An eyewitness from the pleasure boat that rescued Peter Madsen from the sea reports that the "captain" said he had to fix something on board just before the boat sank. This was after Madsen realized that rescue was within reach.

Monday, August 21, 2017

Around 9:00 a.m.: The Copenhagen police publish a press release that says that during the detention hearing, Peter Madsen said that Kim Wall died on board the boat as a result of an accident. After that, he "buried" her at sea. Madsen said he had become depressed as a result of the accident and lay down to sleep on the submarine for a few hours before he got rid of the body.

During the afternoon, the police are called to the southwestern part of Amager Island. A bicyclist has found a dismembered body in the water. During a press conference afterward, the police report that the remains are of a woman but that it cannot be ascertained whether it is the missing woman Kim Wall.

Tuesday, August 22, 2017

The body undergoes a forensic examination and DNA testing.

Wednesday, August 23, 2017

Through Twitter, the Danish police announce that the remains found at Amager belong to Kim Wall. DNA from the journalist's hairbrush and toothbrush match that of the torso that was found. At a press conference, Jens Møller Jensen reports that he had had to tell the family during the early morning hours that the body parts found belonged to Kim Wall. He reveals that someone had inflicted the body with wounds that would prevent it from floating up to the surface. They had found a strap with metal pieces around the body, apparently to weigh down the body and ensure that it would remain on the ocean floor. The forensic report shows that the arms, legs, and head have been intentionally removed from the body. Traces of blood found in the submarine also match the torso's DNA. The autopsy was unable to confirm a cause of death.

Peter Madsen continues to deny the allegations of murder and causing the death of another person.

Tuesday, August 29, 2017

The police conduct a new examination of the submarine. One reason is to look for hidden areas on board.

The examination is done with the help of the Danish Customs Office's special scanner equipment.

Wednesday, August 30, 2017

The examination of the submarine does not yield any results; no areas were found that were not known of before.

Specially trained Swedish dogs, so-called HRD dogs, are assisting Danish police in the search for more remains. The dogs work in shifts, standing at the stern of a small boat, where they hunt for smells from the bottom of the ocean. Together with divers, the search goes along the route that it is believed *UC3 Nautilus* took.

Sunday, September 3, 2017

Madsen requests through his lawyer that the detention hearing scheduled for the coming week be held with open doors. He also demands to be released.

Tuesday, September 5, 2017

Madsen's request is granted, and the hearing takes place with open doors and a massive media presence. It is only the autopsy report that remains confidential. The hearing continues for several hours, and Madsen tells in great detail what had happened on board. He claims that he slipped on the floor in the tower, and that the 150-pound hatch fell and hit Kim Wall in the head. He found her in a pool of blood on the bottom of the boat, and realized she was dead. Madsen is detained for an additional four weeks, now suspected of murder or manslaughter and desecration of a grave.

Madsen does not want to surrender his computer, because he claims it has business secrets. He does not wish to undergo a forensic psychiatric examination, either. The judge rules against Madsen, both regarding the computer and the forensic psychiatric examination.

Tuesday, October 3, 2017

In a new detention hearing, this time Madsen participates through a video link from Vestre Fængsel, where he is imprisoned. The suspicions against him have strengthened, and the material on his computer includes videos containing torture and murder of women. Madsen claims that he is not the only one who has had access to the computer, naming, for example, an intern.

Saturday, October 7, 2017

At a press conference, the Copenhagen police report that several finds were made the day before in Køge Bay—a plastic bag containing Kim Wall's head, another with her clothes and a knife, and two legs. All body parts have been weighted with metal objects in order to keep them from floating up to the surface. There are no fractures to the cranium, which contradicts Madsen's explanation that Kim Wall had been hit in the head with the heavy hatch.

Monday, October 9, 2017

Madsen's DNA is compared to unsolved cases in the Nordic countries since a new EU convention came into force. Countries cooperate by sharing DNA and fingerprints.

Norway is the first to share its records, but no matches turn up.

Wednesday, October 11, 2017

Madsen states that he no longer wishes to cooperate with the police or participate in hearings. He still denies that he has committed murder or violated and dismembered the body.

Thursday, October 12, 2017

A saw is found in Køge Bay along the route that the *UC3 Nautilus* took two months before. The search for Kim Wall's remains continues, although the weather becomes increasingly rough.

Monday, October 30, 2017

It becomes known that Peter Madsen confessed during a hearing that he had cut up Kim Wall's body and thrown parts of it into Køge Bay. He also says that she may have died of carbon monoxide poisoning in the submarine when he himself was up on deck. The definition of the offense is expanded to include sexual crimes under particularly aggravating conditions. A large number of stab wounds in the groin area are the justification for this.

Wednesday, November 1, 2017

Madsen's defense attorney rejects the information that her client had said that a poisoning caused the journalist's death. She has no comment on the fact that he had cut up the body.

The police are of the opinion that Madsen said that it could have been carbon monoxide poisoning, not that he claimed that it was factually so.

Tuesday, November 14, 2017

Through his lawyer, Peter Madsen says that he will stay in jail voluntarily. Thus the detention hearing is rescheduled.

Wednesday, November 22, 2017

The Danish police report than an arm had been found in Køge Bay earlier in the week. It is a left arm that was weighted with the same kind of metal pipe as the body parts found previously.

Wednesday, November 29, 2017

A second arm is found in the same area as the other body parts.

Monday, December 11, 2017

The results of the forensic psychiatric examination are ready and given to the prosecutor. They are not made public.

Tuesday, January 9, 2018

The detention period is extended by another four weeks.

Friday, January 12, 2018

The police end the search for the two missing cell phones.

Tuesday, January 16, 2018

Peter Madsen is indicted. He is charged with murder, sexual crimes, desecration of a grave, and crimes against maritime law.

Thursday, March 8, 2018

The trial begins in the City Court of Copenhagen. A total of twelve trial days are planned for the case. Approximately forty witnesses give testimony during the trial.

Wednesday, April 25, 2018

1:00 p.m.: The judgment is pronounced. Peter Madsen is found guilty of all charges: murder, desecration of a grave, aggravated sexual abuse, and crimes against maritime law. A unanimous court sentences him to life in prison, the harshest punishment under Danish law. Madsen chooses to appeal the sentence immediately to the Eastern High Court. A few days later, Madsen's lawyer reports that Madsen is only appealing the penalty, not the judgment itself.

Wednesday, September 26, 2018

The Eastern High Court upholds the city court's sentence of life imprisonment.

ABOUT THE AUTHORS

Photo © 2017 Perez

Ingrid Wall is a Swedish journalist, author, and mother of journalist Kim Wall. She's worked for more than twenty-five years in the newspaper industry as general assignment reporter, news director, business reporter, and night news editor. In 2000 she was hired as head of communications at Trelleborg Municipality. She is the author of *Trelleborg in the 1950s: City of My Childhood* and *The Beauty of Everyday Language*, and coauthor with her husband, Joachim, of *A Man, an Island, a Life*.

Joachim Wall is a Swedish photojournalist and father of journalist Kim Wall. At the age of fifteen, he had his first photograph—which was of George Harrison—published, and his career was set. After running his own picture agency, in 1985 he started working as a press photographer for the evening paper *Kvällsposten* in Malmö. He went on to cover events big and small, both locally and internationally, for nearly thirty years. He also coauthored a book with his wife, Ingrid, *A Man, an Island, a Life*.

ABOUT THE TRANSLATOR

Photo © 2019 Göran Loman

Born in Painesville, Ohio, into a bilingual family (her father's native language was Finnish), Kathy Saranpa received her bachelor of arts (summa cum laude, Phi Beta Kappa) and master of arts in Scandinavian languages and literature from the University of California, Los Angeles. She defended her dissertation at Yale University under the late George C. Schoolfield, an internationally renowned scholar and translator. She taught translation at the University of Eastern Finland before turning to full-time freelance translation. Dr. Saranpa has lived in Lund, and through her research on the Finland-Swedish writer Ina Lange, has visited Copenhagen many times. Her two children are both professional musicians living in the United States. Dr. Saranpa lives outside Berlin. *A Silenced Voice: The Life of Journalist Kim Wall* is her first published translation.